ACT
on your
BUSINESS

*Braving the Storms of Entrepreneurship
and Creating Success Through
Meaning, Mindset, and Mindfulness*

Lee Chaix McDonough

Contact the author:
www.caravelcoaching.com
www.actonyourbusiness.com

Editing by Jodi Brandon of Jodi Brandon Editorial
Book cover and interior design and typesetting by Lisa Von De Linde of LisaVdesigns
Author photo credit: Photography by Erin Smith

ISBN-13: 978-1-7328736-2-9 (Softcover)
Library of Congress Control Number: 2018911832

Printed in the United States of America

First Edition, February 2019

TABLE OF CONTENTS

LETTER TO THE READER

TO THE INTREPID ENTREPRENEUR—

I see you. Working hard, all day, every day, to bring your dream to life. Devoting countless hours to building your business, spending (way too much) money on the right course, the right program, the right coach—anything that might streamline your path to your dream.

I see you. Posting on Facebook, Pinterest, and Instagram; appearing on guest blogs and podcasts. Creating your content; sharing your story. Perfecting your elevator speech; working out the kinks in your About page; learning the ins-and-outs of copy that converts and sales pages that sell.

I see you. Doing all the right things. Checking all the boxes. Showing up, diving in, giving it your all—and then some. Your drive, your devotion, and your ambition are practically tangible.

I see you. Plagued with self-doubt. Uncertain whether you have what it takes to make this entrepreneurial thing work. Replaying all of your past decisions, your missteps, your mistakes. Vacillating between a mindset of abundance and opportunity, and one of anxiety and self-condemnation. Desperately trying to brave the storms in your business and your life, as the wind swirls and the rain pours.

I see you. I see you, because I am you.

I know all too well what it's like to have a dream, a passion, a desire for something great. When I began my coaching business, I wanted to change the world by connecting with mindful, energized, motivated people who wanted to love their work and their lives. I saw myself, serving people powerfully and changing lives.

Then, shortly after I began, my vision clouded. My aspirations were muted by voices of doubt, comparison, anger, ridicule, and fear. But these weren't the voices of others: They were entirely of my own creation. I dubbed them my inner trolls, who come out to play any and every time I make a move in my business. The more clients I land, the louder they get. The more visible I become, the more they shout me down.

It was exhausting. I felt so helpless and alone, and I seriously wondered whether I was cut out to be an entrepreneur.

And then something amazing happened. Tentatively at first, I started to share my struggles with other people—first my own coach, then other entrepreneurs and small business owners. They responded not with disdain or pity, but with compassion and understanding. They, too, shared the same fears and experienced the same internal racket. They also felt like they were drowning in their own insecurities, despite also believing in their talent and their dream. They, too, felt lonely and alone.

Every person I spoke to shared their own version of not feeling like they were enough: not smart enough, fast enough, interesting enough. They weren't a good enough writer, a good enough public speaker, a good enough businessperson. Deep down, we each feared we didn't have what it takes to be successful, and though the words differed, the message was the same: You are not enough.

Then my intuition stirred, and I remembered how I'd heard this message before—not as a coach or entrepreneur, but in my previous career as a social worker and psychotherapist. I spent more than a decade working with people suffering from mental health–related disorders, including depression, bipolar disorder, anxiety, PTSD, and personality disorders. Though their symptoms varied, they all struggled with their thoughts, feelings, and interpretations, and most had internalized the belief that they were deeply flawed. I'd spent a career helping people battle the same inner trolls that I and my fellow entrepreneurs face, all with a similar message: You are not enough.

With that connection came a jolt of inspiration. What if the strategies that helped my therapy clients could benefit entrepreneurs? What if the evidence-based framework that brought relief in the therapy room could also help small business owners thrive?

And so the idea for this book was born.

As a psychotherapist, I based my work in a powerful therapeutic modality called Acceptance and Commitment Therapy, ACT (pronounced "act") for short. ACT is a modern cognitive-behavioral approach that changes the way we think and behave through meaning, mindset, and mindfulness.

Although the theory behind ACT is extensive, an ACT approach can be best summarized in three simple steps:

1. Accept your current reality (which includes your thoughts, feelings, and experiences).
2. Choose a values-based option.
3. Take action!

The main focus of ACT is to improve a person's psychological flexibility—the ability to be present in the moment, fully aware and open to one's experience, and to act in accordance with our values. Or, to quote psychologist and ACT expert Russ Harris, it's the ability to "be present, open up, and do what matters." Within ACT, there are six core components to psychological flexibility, each with its own shadow side that can limit our flexibility and growth.

Although ACT is first and foremost a therapeutic modality, its basic tenets are universally applicable. And given the entrepreneur's unique constitution—part creator, part innovator, part workhorse, part magician—ACT is particularly relevant and useful.

The more I thought about ACT and entrepreneurship, the more I wondered: What would it look like if we modified the concept of psychological flexibility for an entrepreneurial setting? How would it work to translate the six core components of ACT into the business world and increase one's "entrepreneurial flexibility"?

You're about to find out.

In this book, we'll dive deep into the concept of entrepreneurial flexibility, and I'll introduce you to the six keys to unlocking greater fulfillment, success, and joy. I'll show you how they work together to create a place from which you can bring forth anything you want in your business and your life. I'll address the pitfalls most entrepreneurs fall victim to, and I'll share specific strategies to find your way out.

By the end of this book, you'll have both a road map toward your vision and a backpack full of supplies for the journey. You'll be fully equipped to brave whatever storms surface in your business and your life. And I'll be with you every step of the way.

Are you ready to change your relationship with yourself, grow your business, and transform your life?

Then let's go.

INTRODUCTION

THE FACT THAT you're reading this book suggests a few things about you:

1. You provide incredible experiences for your clients and customers, whether in the form of products or services. You change people's lives for the better through your knowledge and expertise.
2. You're creating or growing your dream business, one that utilizes your talent and energy to make the world a better place. You want your business to be both successful and soul-filled.
3. You haven't totally figured out how to do both at the same time. The demands of small business ownership are clashing with your desire to serve your clients, and you feel pulled between working *in* your business and working *on* your business.

Sound familiar? Good. That means you're in exactly the right place, and you're in good company. Because that was me just a few years ago.

In June 2016, after more than a decade of experience as a social worker and therapist, I switched careers and started Caravel Coaching. Despite having minimal knowledge of or experience in coaching, I knew that I was a damn good therapist who loved helping people, and that I was ready for a profession outside of the traditional medical model. One month after launching my business, I began a coach training program accredited by the International Coach Federation, and I started seeing coaching clients soon after.

Even though I was proficient at coaching, I still felt uncomfortable within my business. I didn't know who I wanted to serve (that elusive "niche") nor how I wanted to coach. All I knew was that I had given up my career as a psychotherapist and had invested a lot of money in a coach training program, and I needed to make this coaching business work.

So I did what I usually do: I researched my way through it. I read all the books, listened to all the podcasts, and invested way too much money in online courses promising to help me create a profitable business. I did everything a good entrepreneur is supposed to do: I created a business plan, developed a marketing strategy, and got out there and hustled. Networking, website, email list, guest blogs, workshops, presentations—you name it, I did it. Yet even though I had a few paying clients, I still felt like I wasn't doing it right. I felt like I was "playing" at business, and I couldn't figure out what I was doing wrong.

Hindsight being what it is, it's now painfully obvious just where I went wrong. Sure, I had a solid action plan. But that plan wasn't anchored in my values; it was anchored in fear. *I gave up my career and invested a lot of money. I need to make this coaching business work.* All of the plans and decisions I'd been making for my business had nothing to do with what mattered most to me. They were entirely fear-based, concerned solely with making sure I hadn't sacrificed my time, energy, money, and career for a pipe dream.

Even though I'd been working as an Acceptance and Commitment Therapy (ACT) therapist and knew all about meaning, mindset, and mindfulness, I didn't make the link between these key ACT concepts and my business. And damn if that didn't hurt. It's a terribly humbling experience to recognize you have a blind spot, and I had a big one: When it came to my business, I wasn't practicing what I preached, and I felt completely humiliated. There I was, the ACT expert, building a business based on fear. No wonder I felt like an imposter.

One year into my business, I essentially started over and embarked on a journey of entrepreneurial self-discovery. I needed to know what mattered most to me as a business owner—what gave my business and my life meaning—so that I could take true action in my business. I engaged in some deep introspection to get clear on my business core values, and discovered that some of my values from my years as a therapist were still relevant, such as service, empowerment, and connection. But now that I was an entrepreneur, other new values emerged, like autonomy and innovation. As I wrote down what mattered most to me as a coach and entrepreneur, I developed a deeper understanding about how my business informed my sense of purpose and meaning, and vice versa.

I also went back to basics to figure out what it meant to have an entrepreneurial mindset. I was familiar with the concept of mindset from my work as an ACT therapist and as a resilience trainer for the United States Air Force, so I applied that knowledge to how I viewed myself as a business owner. I saw how my limiting beliefs, negative self-talk, and emotional avoidance kept me stuck and led to fear-based decision-making, and I recognized that I had the tools to reshape my mindset.

Finally, I returned to mindfulness, head hung low and tail between my legs. A few years earlier, my mindfulness practice was thriving, and included daily meditation and a "live-in-the-now" approach to life. But as the stressors of small business ownership mounted, my mindful approach to life waned and was quickly overtaken by worries about the future and regrets about the past. I saw how losing connection with the present moment compromised my self-awareness and made it difficult for me to feel connected to or fulfilled by my business. But when I approached my business and my life in the moment, the anxiety and fear lessened.

Through meaning, mindset, and mindfulness, I rediscovered who I really was and how I wanted to show up in my business. I rewrote my business plan, refreshed my branding, and redesigned my website. With a new, solid strategy rooted in what mattered most, I implemented my action plan and my business started to grow. I was making more connections, fostering more relationships, and ultimately gaining more clients. I felt at home in my business. I finally felt like I belonged.

Most importantly, I was ready the next time the storms of entrepreneurship showed up—because there was another storm, and there will be storms again. Whether it's a website crash, a supplier screwing up a big order, an angry client, the one certainty in business is uncertainty, and shit happens. But because I've anchored my business in meaning, mindset, and mindfulness, I'm braving any storms that come my way with calm, compassion, and courage.

This is what I want for you. I want you to have a business that lights you up, one that you love working in and working on. I want you to feel solid in the knowledge of what makes you *you*, and how that translates into a successful, profitable, and fulfilling business. And I want you to believe that you have what it takes to handle anything life throws at you—because you do. I know it's possible because I've seen it happen, not just in my life, but in the lives of my clients too.

Within the pages of this book, you will find a road map for your expedition to build your entrepreneurial flexibility. You'll create a different way of relating to yourself and your mind while discovering what it means to build a business and life built on meaning, mindset, and mindfulness. You'll learn about the six core processes of psychological and entrepreneurial flexibility, why each is important when building a successful business, and techniques to implement them in your business and your life.

And the best part is, you won't be alone. I'll be here with you and for you, on every page and at every step. I want this book to help you create the business of your dreams, which is why I've also created additional resources for you on the book's website (https://www.actonyourbusiness.com).

You have everything you need to build a successful business you love, and this is your guidebook for the journey. You got this.

WELCOME
TO YOUR
MIND

CHAPTER 1

The Mind

THROUGHOUT THIS BOOK, you're going to hear me talk about "the mind" a lot. Like, *a lot*. That's because how we understand and relate to the mind is an essential component of ACT and entrepreneurial flexibility. So before we get too much further, let's go over what "the mind" is, and what it's not. Trust me: The rest of the book will make *so* much more sense if we do.

BRAIN VS. MIND

First, we need to think about the brain and the mind as two separate things. The brain is an organ in your body. It handles just about all of your body's physical actions, whether consciously or unconsciously. It is responsible for almost everything your physical body does: managing your heart rate and your breathing, controlling the major organ systems, fostering cell growth, regulating hormones. When you think about everything the brain is responsible for, it's . . . well, it's mind-blowing.

So while the brain handles your physical self, the mind is something else entirely. It's not a part of the body the way an organ like the brain is, yet it's an instrumental part of who we are. You can't identify the mind in a person the way you can a femur or an eardrum, and yet, everyone has one. The mind is everything and not a thing, all at once. (I know. Deep, right?)

Often, when I'm trying to wrap my mind around a difficult concept, it helps to start with a simple definition. According to the *Oxford Dictionary*, the first definition of the word *mind* is "the element of a person that enables them to be aware of the world and their experiences, to think, and to feel; the faculty of consciousness and thought." That's a good start, but *Merriam-Webster* takes it even further: "a) the element or complex of elements in an individual that feels, perceives, thinks, wills, and especially reasons; b) the conscious mental events and capabilities in an organism; c) the organized conscious and unconscious adaptive mental ability of an organism."

I know quoting not just one, but two, dictionaries probably isn't super exciting stuff, but stay with me. Both of these definitions address two main concepts that are not only important components of the mind, but are also critical aspects of entrepreneurial flexibility. First, the mind includes your innermost experiences, things that others are not necessarily privy to. This includes your thoughts, your feelings, your memories, your urges, your perceptions, and your desires. All of these things feel very real to you, but I wouldn't necessarily know you had them unless you communicated them to me somehow. They are internal, they are private, and they are constant.

The second concept that both definitions share is that of consciousness. The easiest way to describe consciousness is your awareness. In this case, it's your awareness of your innermost experiences. It's the extent to which you are aware of your thoughts, feelings, memories, and so on, as well as the effect they have on your subsequent internal experiences *and* your outward behaviors.

The reason I prefer the *Merriam-Webster* definition is its third component: the "adaptive mental ability" part. This suggests that we each have the ability to modify how we relate and respond to our internal experiences, and our level of awareness is at the heart of creating that change. In essence, you are able to use your mind to change your mind. (Does it get any more meta than that?)

What an encouraging and empowering concept! And that's what this book is all about: how to raise your awareness and recognize the influence your mind has on your life, so that you can assume responsibility for your perspective and develop greater mental (and entrepreneurial) flexibility. With increased flexibility comes freedom— freedom from the messages your mind feeds you, freedom to see opportunities in challenges, freedom to create the business and the life you want.

YOUR MIND: THE GOOD, THE BAD, AND THE UGLY

If you're like most people, you probably have a love-hate relationship with your mind. On one hand, your mind is an extraordinary creation and capable of so many amazing things. Not only does it help you learn and reason, but it has developed incredible mechanisms to keep you safe and help you thrive. The three qualities of the mind— internal experience, consciousness, and flexibility—are what set humans apart from other animals. Your mind is truly remarkable.

And yet, the mind can also be your worst nightmare. It can terrorize you with terrible thoughts, disgusting images, awful memories, and horrible feelings. It can convince you that you are nothing, you are insignificant, you are unworthy. It can smother you in shame and engulf you in rage. In short, your mind can torture you and make your life a living hell. So what's a savvy entrepreneur to do?

First, take comfort in the fact that this is a normal, albeit infuriating, process. Almost everyone experiences these emotional ups and downs, so you're not alone. Second, realize that you are capable of creating change, and that includes the relationship you have with your mind. I know it may seem difficult, and that's understandable; after all, we're talking about forging new neural pathways and changing ingrained behaviors that have served you for decades. But just because it's difficult doesn't mean it's impossible. It can be done, and this book shows you how.

In fact, just by reading this book, you've already started the process. A few pages ago, you started to view the mind as something separate from you, as a part of you but not all of you. That awareness is the first step toward harnessing your power and making your mind work for you. Everything we talk about in this book begins with that awareness. So don't for a moment think you can't change—because you already have.

That awareness is just the beginning. This book provides you with valuable information and actionable processes to help you strengthen the connection you have with yourself, your work, and your world. I teach you how to approach your business in an entirely new way, one rooted in a deep knowledge of who you are and how you are meant to contribute to the world. You're about to learn more about how meaning, mindset, and mindfulness work together to increase your mental flexibility and your resilience, allowing you to create more success in your business and fulfillment in your life. And who doesn't want that?

CHAPTER 2

The 3 Ms

WHEN I STARTED MY BUSINESS, I knew a lot about how to serve people, but very little about running a business. So I did what I always do when I'm faced with a new-to-me issue: I research it. I bought books, read blog posts, listened to podcasts, completed free five-day challenges, and immersed myself in all things business. By the time I finally got things started, I had essentially received an MBA from the School of Life.

But as with many degrees, you graduate with a lot of knowledge about what to do, but not necessarily with a lot of experience. So there I was, with a business plan that looked great on paper. I had chosen my audience, created my ICA (ideal client avatar), identified a niche, researched my client's pain points, figured out a solution, and crafted a beautiful 15-second elevator pitch to describe myself and my business. I had done it all, just like the experts had recommended.

And yet even though I had followed all the rules and checked all the boxes, something felt off. Caravel Coaching had a nice web page, a great logo, and a clear message—but Lee Chaix McDonough was nowhere in it. In my effort to create a client-centered business, I had focused 100% of my energy and resources on the client and left myself out of the equation. I had a business that looked good on paper but didn't feel like me at all.

I don't mean to suggest that you shouldn't focus on your clients' needs; you absolutely should. But before you start building a business around your ideal client, you need to make sure your business reflects you—your values, your vision, and your goals. The more you infuse your true self in your business, the more you draw your ideal clients to you.

So how do you do that? How do you build a business that serves your clients powerfully while authentically demonstrating what matters most to you? You do that by starting with the 3 Ms: meaning, mindset, and mindfulness. The 3 Ms are the foundation of the six core processes, which I introduce in Chapter 4 and go even deeper into in Section Two. But first, let's look at each of the 3 Ms and how they work together to create a business that speaks to your clients while reflecting who you are.

MEANING

I have an important question for you.

Why did you buy this book?

Maybe you picked it up because you want to learn more about building a business you love without losing your mind. Perhaps you're intrigued about the business applications of meaning and mindfulness. Maybe the phrase *creating success* in the subtitle caught your eye. Or maybe you're my mother and you bought it to show your support. (Thanks, Mom!)

No matter why you invested in this book, there's an underlying reason that supported your decision, and that reason is linked to your values. So if you bought this book because you want to create a sustainable business you love without sacrificing your sanity, then I would guess that you value peace, balance (especially that elusive "work-life balance"), and love. If you're interested in exploring new ways of applying mindfulness in business, I would infer that you value mindful living and innovation. If you're seeking strategies you can use to support your clients while growing your business, then you probably value service and success. And if you're my mom, you value family and love.

Every action you take (or choose not to take) tells a story about what matters most to you. Every decision you make (or don't make) informs who you are. When you're acting in harmony with your values, then your choices reflect that alignment—and man, does being aligned feel good! When you're consistent in your beliefs, words, and deeds, then you foster a sense of meaning that comes from living an authentic life.

While each of us may have different values, that doesn't mean one of us is right and the other is wrong. It simply indicates that we hold different priorities when it comes to how we choose to live our lives. That's because values are inherently objective: They're not good or bad; they're neutral. One person may value empathy, service, and opportunity, whereas another may value adventure, innovation, and productivity. Neither approach to business or life is right or wrong. It's just the lens through which that person views the world and gives meaning to their life.

Now, that's not to say having different values doesn't create problems. When values clash, it definitely creates tension and even conflict, both with others and within ourselves. If you place a high value on efficiency and productivity, you might be more apt to make decisions quickly in order to get the job done. But if your business partner or client leads with creativity and partnership as values, then she might take longer to make decisions because she's exploring multiple options and getting feedback from key stakeholders. Each of your underlying values leads to different approaches, and if you're not aware of and communicating about these differences, then there's going to be stress.

It's also common to experience an internal value clash. For example, two of my core values are service and love. Service is a huge part of my coaching practice, and I take great pride in serving my clients powerfully. I want to show up for them and support them every step of their journey, and I've built my business on providing a high level of service. I also value love, which shows up throughout my life, but particularly in my relationships with my family. Nothing brings me a sense of connection and fulfillment like being present in the moment with my husband and children. I love spending time with them, and being a partner and a mother is an integral part of my identity.

So what happens during the summer, when my children are out of school and want to have fun adventures, but I still have a business to run? Hello, value clash! I wind up feeling torn between spending time with my kids and showing up for my clients, and my passion to serve runs head-on into my desire to love. For the first week or two of every summer, I'm scattered and can't shake this sense of low-lying frenetic, chaotic energy. It's an undercurrent in almost everything I do, and it's my personal warning sign that I'm experiencing a value clash.

Just as awareness and communication are critical to navigating value clashes between people, they are also the key to dealing with an inner value clash. When I sense that frenetic energy, I know it's time to stop and check in with myself. It's almost like taking my psychological pulse, with the result being greater awareness about what's causing my struggle. Once I'm aware of it, I can do something about it. I can have a little conversation with myself about what happens when I try to do everything perfectly, which leads me to create boundaries for work and home.

While serving my clients and running my business are important to me, I remind the service-oriented part of me that I don't want the needs of others to run my life. I also remind the part of myself that values love of the benefits of having school-age children. Because they are more self-sufficient than toddlers and preschoolers, they are fully capable of entertaining themselves for a couple of hours while I get some work done. So in the summer, mornings are for work and afternoons are for family. Sometimes I make exceptions for each, but they usually balance out.

Although value clashes are uncomfortable, they teach us a lot about what matters most and what we're willing to do to live a purposeful life. When navigated mindfully, these clashes create space for opportunity, allowing us to foster a sense of connection and meaning, both within ourselves and in our relationships with family, friends, clients, colleagues, and the world.

Living a values-consistent life also creates an energy that others sense and that connects them to you. For example, think about a person in your life who you feel connected to. There's likely a deep level of trust inherent in that relationship, and that trust stems from their authenticity. They may not have ever told you what matters most to them, but if asked, you could probably identify the core values around which they've built their life, and you could provide evidence of their behavior to support your observations.

This sense of trust that comes with value consistency isn't just for individuals. It's for brands and businesses too. There's a fundamental concept in marketing that says a client or customer needs three things before they're willing to buy your product or service: First, they need to know you, then they need to like you, and finally, they need to trust you. That's the "know like trust" (KLT) factor, and without a strong KLT factor, a business won't survive. So how does a business develop high KLT? By connecting with clients from a values-based perspective—first by sharing knowledge (what does your business do?), then by building affinity (what values do we share?), and finally by building trust (what's the evidence that your product/service represents our shared values?).

This is why it's imperative that an entrepreneur know what her values are and how they show up in her business. When you know what matters to you and allow that to inform your business, you're creating a deeper sense of meaning for both you and your clients. Your clients feel connected to you, because they are buying more than just your product or service. They are investing in the experience and the meaning you co-create.

But what if you don't know what your values are? Or what if you have an idea about what's important to you, but you don't know how to translate that to your business? Then you are in the right place, my friend. In a few chapters, I introduce you to two core processes that directly address how to create meaning in your business and your life through your values, and we dive even deeper into how to do it in Section Two. But we need to cover two other concepts first, so let's keep moving!

MINDSET

Over the last decade or so, we've been paying more attention to how our thoughts can influence and even create the experiences we have. We've seen this popularized through concepts such as the Law of Attraction and in books that promote manifesting what you want through intention setting and positive thinking. But these ideas do not belong solely to the realm of New Age and self-help; the truth is, psychologists have been studying this idea for years, with much of their work based the concept of *mindset*.

In 2006, Carol Dweck published her book *Mindset* and revolutionized the way people view their abilities. In the book, Dr. Dweck proposes that a person's mindset, or how a person views their talents and abilities, has significant ramifications on their happiness and success. She suggests that people generally fall into one of two categories—those with fixed mindsets and those with growth mindsets—and suggests that by cultivating a growth mindset, we open ourselves up to new possibilities and incredible results.

The key determining factor in what kind of mindset you have lies in how you view your talents, abilities, and intelligence. If you believe these qualities are static or unchanging, then you're more likely to have a fixed mindset, whereas if you believe someone can develop or improve their talents, abilities, and intelligence, then you're more likely to have a growth mindset. Your mindset shapes not only your beliefs about yourself, but also about the world around you.

For example, many of my clients are mental health therapists looking to grow their private practices. In the past, therapists didn't have to worry too much about marketing; they were able to fill their appointments based off of insurance lists or referrals from doctors. However, as more clinicians enter the field and as insurance coverage changes, many therapists are finding that in order to have a thriving practice, they need to beef up their marketing efforts.

One of my coaching clients was very resistant to this changing environment, and many of our sessions focused on her anger, frustration, and anxiety about having to step up her marketing. "I didn't go to school to be a salesperson," she said. "I went to school to help people. I'm just not good at sales. I don't like it and I don't want to do it." It was extraordinarily difficult for her to adapt, and she truly believed she didn't have what it takes to be successful in private practice. In this area of her life, she presented with more of a fixed mindset.

Another client of mine had a different outlook. While she also had some anxiety about being more proactive in her marketing, she was able to adapt fairly quickly. "One of the things about being a therapist is that you're really good at establishing relationships and connecting with people quickly," she said. "In a way, that should make me really good at marketing. It's just a different way of building a relationship with someone." Even though marketing a private practice was initially outside her skill set, she was able to find the opportunity in the challenge and to identify how her current strengths could help her moving forward. She exhibited a growth mindset.

Dweck's research suggests that when people adopt fixed mindsets, they are more likely to avoid challenges because of the risk of failure. In general, they tend to minimize or ignore feedback, and are apt to disregard new information or approaches to accomplishing a task. (The saying *If it ain't broke, don't fix it* was probably created by someone with a fixed mindset.) As a result, people with fixed mindsets tend to be sensitive to criticism and fearful of making mistakes. This can wreak havoc on their confidence, and create anxiety and a sense of unfulfillment.

People with growth mindsets, on the other hand, are much more likely to welcome challenges and are less likely to view adverse outcomes as failures. Their focus is not on validation, but on mastery. They are able to separate their sense of identity from the task at hand. They know what they do doesn't define who they are. As a result, they are open to feedback and generally learn from their experiences (particularly the unsuccessful ones), adapting their approach for the next time.

Now, in reality, no one's mindset is completely fixed or completely growth-oriented. In fact, I prefer to think of mindset as a spectrum, and at any given time, we fall somewhere on that spectrum. In some areas, perhaps we're more fixed, while in others, we're more growth-oriented. Our mindset may be influenced by situations, people, or circumstances, so it's possible to move around on that spectrum quite a bit. Thus, part of the challenge is to recognize when we're falling into a fixed mindset, so that we can mindfully shift our thinking more toward growth.

Did you catch that? About mindfully shifting our thinking toward growth? I want to focus on that for a minute, because there are two important points there worth highlighting. The first is that it is possible to change your mindset. You're not born with either a fixed or growth-oriented mindset that you're stuck with forever. You can develop a growth mindset by reframing how you view failure and challenges, and by looking for the opportunity in setback, you're shifting into a growth mindset.

Second, mindfulness and mindset are highly correlated. As you develop greater awareness of yourself and how your mind works, you become more flexible, more resilient, and more growth-oriented. Mindfulness practice changes your mindset, so that you're able not only to accomplish more, but to feel more fulfilled while doing it. So on that note, let's dive into this concept of mindfulness and explore what it means to approach your business—and your life—from a mindful perspective.

MINDFULNESS

As I mentioned in the Introduction, everything you're about to read is based in the tenets of Acceptance and Commitment Therapy, or ACT for short. ACT is considered a third-wave cognitive behavioral therapy (CBT), which simply means it's a newer form of CBT that's anchored in mindfulness. Mindfulness is the thread that connects everything in this book, so now that we're clear on what the mind is and how it operates, I want to dive into what mindfulness is, what it isn't, and why it's so damn important.

I'll be honest: When I first started learning about mindfulness more than a decade ago, the first thing that came to my mind was an image of a yogi on a mountaintop, seated in lotus position, fingers making the OK sign. My experience was pretty common back then. Mindfulness was just starting to gain popularity, and it wasn't well understood by the general public.

Today, mindfulness is a far more accepted practice—and yet there are still many misconceptions about what mindfulness is and what it's not. For example, many people think practicing mindfulness means stopping your thoughts or completely clearing your mind. That is not mindfulness—not even close. Not only is that not mindfulness, it's not realistic and likely not even possible.

So let me tell you what mindfulness is. Actually, let me let psychologist and mindfulness expert Jon Kabat-Zinn tell you, because his definition is the simplest, most elegant one I've come across:

Mindfulness is awareness that arises through paying attention, on purpose, in the present moment, non-judgmentally.[1]

In essence, mindfulness is the act of paying attention with intention, purpose, and non-judgment. There's nothing about not thinking or having a blank mind. In fact, mindfulness expects us to have thoughts, and provides us with a way of acknowledging those thoughts—with intention, purpose, and non-judgment.

Sometimes, the concepts of mindfulness and meditation get confused with each other, and people often believe they're the same thing. Because these two concepts are frequently paired together, it might seem like you can't have one without the other—but that's not true. Meditation can be a mindfulness practice (and in Chapter 11 I provide you with some examples of how to engage in mindfulness meditation). However, you don't have to meditate to practice mindfulness, and there are other ways than meditation to pay attention to the moment. While meditation is an extraordinarily beneficial practice, it's not a requirement for mindfulness—so if it's not your thing, no worries.

No matter how you choose to practice it, the heart of mindfulness is showing up and being present with intention, purpose, and non-judgment. Let's take a closer look at each of those three components.

Intention

Paying attention with intention is about being deliberate and thoughtful in how you relate to your thoughts, as opposed to the default mode most of us rely on, in which we buy into our thoughts and attach to them. I go into this default mode in more detail in Chapter 9 but for now, just know that mindfulness asks us to approach our thoughts differently. Rather than accepting our thoughts as truth and getting caught up in them, mindfulness encourages us to redirect our attention to the world around us or within us.

For example, I can be paying attention to what's going on in the outside world, like the silhouette created by a tree branch against the sky, or how it feels as I sip my coffee and it flows over my tongue and down the back of my throat. Or I can be paying attention to my inner world, like the feel of my ribcage expanding as I breathe in. I intentionally direct my attention into every detail in my environment, which creates distance from the mental chatter and grounds me in the present moment.

Purpose

The second component of mindfulness is purpose. This gets into not just the act of paying attention, but the reason we are paying attention: to stay in the present moment and to live and invest fully in the present moment. Purpose goes hand in hand with intention, because when you're fully present in the moment, you're more connected to yourself, to the people you're with, to the work you're doing, and to what matters most to you. It connects you to your big why, which we'll talk about later in the book.

Non-Judgment

In my opinion, the most difficult part of mindfulness is non-judgment because it goes against our most basic, primal instincts. For this reason, I'm going to go into a bit more detail than I did with intention and purpose.

As humans, we're hard-wired not only to pay attention to our surroundings but to make judgments about them, which is why we've survived for millennia. Our minds allowed us to evaluate our environment and to form opinions and judgments, which kept us safe and allowed our species to survive and thrive. In this sense, the mind became this ever-present, always-on safety monitor, helping us determine whether to fight, flee, freeze, or operate as usual.

But here's the thing: Even though our society has evolved, the mind really hasn't. We still have that reptilian brain that processes all threats the same way, and the mind responds accordingly. It doesn't differentiate between the saber-toothed tiger or the pillaging and plundering invaders, and the obnoxious boss or the looming dead-line. All are viewed as threats that need to be mitigated.

But the mind isn't limited to just matters of safety and security. It formulates opinions and makes judgments even when we're safe, because that's our default process and usually we don't even realize we're doing it. We see someone and we automatically size them up. (*Her dress is cute. Those shoes are heinous. He looks like a nice guy. Seriously, what is with those shoes?*) The judgment factory converts observations to judgments and churns them out continuously.

The judgment factory is not limited to the external world. It's an internal process as well, which can be particularly damaging. The inner critic (I call mine my inner troll) can push the judgment factory into mandatory overtime. (*That was the wrong thing to say. I'm such an idiot. What is wrong with me? If only I were thinner/smarter/taller/younger/better.*) These ruminations affect our behavior, and we go on judgment over-load, which affects our ability to connect with others and ourselves.

This is why approaching mindfulness from a place of non-judg-ment is so critical—and so difficult. We can approach our thoughts with a sense of curiosity and openness, so that when those thoughts arise (and they will arise), we stop the judgment factory. We don't fall into our default tendency to buy into the thought, but instead we simply notice what's happening. Instead of thinking, *Oh, I shouldn't be having that thought,* or even, *Why am I having that thought?* it becomes, *Oh look, I'm having a thought.* No judgment, no meaning. Just noticing.

To illustrate this point, here's an entirely hypothetical example that has never happened to me before ever:

> *I text my BFF to make plans for the weekend. A few hours go by without a response. I know she has her phone with her, because she's posting on Facebook and Instagram. She literally just Snapped five minutes ago, but didn't send it to me. Is she pissed at me? Oh God, I bet she's pissed at me. Why is she pissed at me? What did I do? God, I'm a terrible friend. I don't even know what I did to make her angry.*

Hello, shame spiral! A simple observation (she hasn't texted me back) turns into full-on judgment (she's angry with me and I'm a terrible friend). Let's see what happens when we bring mindfulness into the mix.

> *I text my BFF to make plans for the weekend. A few hours go by without a response. I know she has her phone with her, because she's posting on Facebook and Instagram. How curious—I'm having the feelings of anxiety and worry, and I'm having the thought that she's angry with me. Look how my mind is starting to create a story about what's happening. Wow.*

In the second example, I'm still having the same distressing thoughts and feelings. But instead of allowing them to dictate my response, I just notice them with curiosity. I make space for them, which allows me to be open to new ways of perceiving what's going on. This is a much more compassionate approach; I'm not beating myself up for being a bad friend or for having the thoughts in the first place.

The truth is, practicing non-judgment is simple but not easy. We're going against the mind's default tendency to judge, which can feel foreign or uncomfortable, like wearing your right shoe on your left foot. This is why it's called mindfulness practice: It really does take practice to approach our thoughts with openness, curiosity, and distance. But when we do, it can revolutionize the way we show up in our businesses, the way we work with clients, and the way we relate to others and ourselves.

MOVING FORWARD

Okay, so mindfulness is paying attention with intention, purpose, and non-judgment. Got it. Sounds good. But now what? How do we actually put this into practice—and why is it so important that we do this whole mindfulness thing, anyway?

These are important questions, and we go into the why in Chapter 6, in which you learn how to blend meaning, mindset, and mindfulness into what I call entrepreneurial flexibility, and I walk you through the how in Chapter 11. But first, I want to first introduce you to the core processes in ACT and what it means to be psychologically flexible, and then we get into specific techniques you can use to increase your success and happiness.

In the chapters that follow, you learn the basic tenets behind ACT, the six core processes that make up psychological flexibility, and their corresponding shadow processes. You discover what it means to have entrepreneurial flexibility, and I teach you the three key questions to ask yourself in order to clarify your vision and purpose. Then, in Section Two, we dive deep into each of the core processes, and I show you the tools and strategies to help you incorporate meaning, mindset, and mindfulness into your business—and your life.

The rest of this book will change how you relate to yourself, your business, and the world around you. I'll be your guide every step of the way, so when you're ready, let's go.

CHAPTER 3

Let's Get Flexible

TIME FOR A QUICK RECAP. You now know the difference between the brain and the mind, and how the mind both helps and hinders you. You know why it's so important to get clear on your purpose and your values. You know what it means when we talk about mindset, and how developing a growth mindset can help you achieve greater personal and professional success. And you understand how mindfulness, or being in the present moment in an objective, non-judgmental frame of mind, is critical to cultivating a greater sense of fulfillment in your work and in your life.

Wow—that's a lot! You deserve a break. Go grab a glass of wine/cup of coffee/mug of your beverage of choice, take a quick stretch, then come back.

I'm serious. Self-care is important. I'll wait.

Okay, all good? Great. Here we go.

The six core processes you're about to learn work together to create what I call "entrepreneurial flexibility." Entrepreneurial flexibility is largely based on the concept of psychological flexibility, the cornerstone of Acceptance and Commitment Therapy (ACT). Because ACT and psychological flexibility are the foundation of entrepreneurial flexibility, the 3 Ms, and the six core processes, it's important that you have a clear understanding of psychological flexibility and the basic tenets of ACT. I use my own professional and personal experience with ACT to introduce you to the basic concepts, and I don't get too heavy on the theory or the psycho-jargon, I promise!

Let's start with psychological flexibility. What on earth does that mean? Russ Harris, a well-respected ACT psychologist and an author of several books on ACT, defines psychological flexibility as "the ability to be in the present moment with full awareness and openness to our experience, and to take action guided by our values."[2] As a therapeutic process, ACT seeks to increase a person's psychological flexibility.

This might sound a little familiar. In Chapter 2, we explored present-moment awareness and openness to experience as core mindfulness principles. This is why ACT is categorized with other mindfulness-oriented approaches, such as mindfulness-based cognitive therapy (MBCT) and dialectical behavior therapy (DBT).

As an ACT-trained therapist, I've witnessed my clients transform their lives by increasing their psychological flexibility, and I know firsthand how ACT can be a life changer for people who live with depression, anxiety, post-traumatic stress disorder, and a host of other mental health conditions. I believe the reason ACT is such a powerful treatment modality is because of its focus on improving the quality of your life, rather than on reducing your symptoms (though symptom reduction is often the result). One of the bedrock principles of ACT is that our clients are not broken. Rather, they're stuck. And ACT helps get people unstuck.

In 2009, I had an incredible opportunity to complete a six-month traineeship through the Department of Veterans Affairs, during which I studied and practiced the fundamentals of ACT while receiving supervision from an ACT mentor. One of the most important things I learned was that to be an effective ACT practitioner, I had to implement the skills and processes in my own life. I had to practice what I preached. So during my traineeship, I devoted myself to the practice of ACT, applying the principles of psychological flexibility and the six core processes to my own life while also using the modality with my clients. It was an incredible experience to grow alongside my clients, and to live through my own personal transformation while they lived through theirs.

Though I lived through a particularly difficult bout of depression as a teenager, I've been fortunate that depression has been largely absent in my adult life. Yet even though I wasn't depressed during this time, my ACT practice still led to significant improvements in my mood, my energy, and my level of connection to myself and to the world around me. I discovered that the benefits of ACT aren't just for people currently dealing with mental illness; they are available to anyone and everyone.

This revelation was particularly important in the summer of 2015, when my family and I moved back to the United States after living in Europe for four years. My husband had just separated from the Air Force, we were negotiating the purchase of what would become his dental practice, and he, our two sons, and I were negotiating the transition from military to civilian life. It was a chaotic, lonely time, and I felt completely unmoored. I was homesick for my adopted country of Germany, and I felt like a stranger in the States. So much had changed since we had left in 2011, and I was experiencing severe reverse culture shock. The first few months were so difficult, and I felt more distant and disconnected from myself than ever before.

Then one day, when I was feeling particularly lonely and alone, I had a spark of insight. I picked up my copy of *The Happiness Trap* by Russ Harris and refamiliarized myself with ACT and the six core processes. Although I wasn't depressed, I was certainly at risk, and I knew in my gut that rebuilding my psychological flexibility was the first step in healing. ACT was my touchstone throughout my first year back in the US, and the six core processes helped me regain my footing and take my next steps.

A year later, with the struggles of transition largely behind me, I started Caravel Coaching and entered the world of entrepreneurship. Though I had completed a coach training program and knew how to work *in* my business as a coach, I had no idea how to work *on* my business as an owner. My first year with Caravel felt like one long crash course in marketing, sales, social media, web design, accounting, blogging, and networking. Even though I loved the challenge of developing my entrepreneurial muscles, it was an incredibly taxing year that left me feeling drained and uncertain. I was falling into the comparison trap, looking at other coaches and wishing I was as confident and successful as they were. Though I knew I had accomplished a lot in that first year, it didn't seem like enough. *I* didn't seem like enough.

I realized that during the first year of my business, I had spent almost all of my time trying to fit the mold of what I thought a coach "should" be, rather than honoring who I am. This was evident in my branding, my website, and how I interacted with my clients. I wanted so badly to do everything right and be like everyone else that I lost myself along the way.

Again, I returned to ACT and the six core processes. I identified the mental traps I set for myself and I began to dismantle them. I extended myself grace and compassion, and I regained my sense of agency and self-determination. This time, as I practiced the processes, I began to intentionally infuse them into my business and my brand, so that Caravel Coaching would be an authentic manifestation of my soul's purpose. I approached everything about my business from an ACT perspective, something that felt familiar while working in my business coaching my clients (after all, my ACT experience started with my therapy clients), yet felt revolutionary while working on my business as an owner.

Although ACT is a therapeutic process, it lends itself naturally to the entrepreneurial space. In fact, I didn't truly understand the power and potential ACT had to change the world until I applied the processes in a business context. The philosophy of ACT and the six core processes have now become an integral part of who I am and how I relate to the world around me. ACT changed my mindset, improved my business, and—I say this without reservation—forever transformed my life.

That's why you're holding this book in your hands. I believe that building psychological and entrepreneurial flexibility is the key to creating a successful and fulfilling life. Not only do I use the six core processes professionally and personally, I help my clients do the same in theirs, with extraordinary results. And now it's your turn.

CHAPTER 4

The Six Core Processes

THE SIX CORE PROCESSES that comprise psychological flexibility create the foundation for a fulfilling life *and* for a successful and profitable business. There is no set order to the processes; you can start with any of them, and you'll find they all work together to enhance each other and build your flexibility.

Because the six processes are so intertwined, it helps to know the basics about all of them before we go into each one in depth. So in this chapter, I briefly explain what each process means and why it's important. We dive deeper into each process in Section Two, where I guide you through how to use them to up-level your business and enrich your life.

As much as I love ACT, as with almost every psychological approach, the jargon can be confusing and overwhelming. It's a pet peeve of mine, because jargon alienates people and makes things far more complicated than they need to be. So, I've renamed the core processes for the entrepreneurial space (as shown in the following chart), with the intention of making these processes more accessible and applicable.

The Six Core Processes of Entrepreneurial and Psychological Flexibility	
Core Processes of Entrepreneurial Flexibility	**Core Processes of Psychological Flexibility**
Determine What Matters	Values
Make it So	Committed Action
Create Space	Cognitive Defusion
Let it Be	Acceptance
Anchor Yourself	Contact with the Present Moment
Observe Yourself	Self-as-Context

DETERMINE WHAT MATTERS

The first core process we'll explore is **Determine What Matters**, or in ACT language, your Values. Since the inception of ACT, the word *values* has become increasingly popular in the context of knowing what's important to you, and with good reason. Being clear on your values is key in business and life, and when we connect what is important to us with the work that we do, we find greater satisfaction.

However, because the word *values* has become more mainstream, its popularity has diluted its meaning. It's easy to hear the word *values* and gloss over it, thinking, "Yeah, yeah, I know all about this already." But even those of us who are familiar with the concept of values would do well to pause and fully engage with this question: What matters most to you? Throughout this book, I use *values* and *what matters most* interchangeably.

Determining what matters most is the basis of having a satisfying, fulfilling, meaningful life. When you know what's most important to you, you can use that knowledge to inform your behaviors and achieve what you want. It may be helpful to think of what matters most to you as your compass; it shows you what direction to go to achieve what you want.

Determine What Matters requires you to ask and answer some pretty big questions: What do you want your life to be about? In your heart, or in your soul, what do you want to bring forth in your life? When all is said and done, what really matters? Some of my clients have ready answers to these questions, and others don't. If the answers don't come easily to you, don't worry. That's normal, and this book will help you clarify your values.

In fact, thinking about what you desire most can help you Determine What Matters. When you ask, "What do I desire most?" your response is closely related to what you value. Take a moment to ask yourself, "What do I want or desire most in this world?" Here are some possible answers:

- A partner/spouse
- A job I love
- Money
- A house I love
- To travel more
- Children
- To lose weight

Each of these desires have an underlying value underneath. For example, someone who desires a partner may place high value on partnership, or romance, or love. Someone who seeks money may hold financial security, material comforts, or independence to be of high importance. Someone who wants to travel more may cite freedom, adventure, and knowledge (of other cultures) as their guiding principles. You can see that with each desire comes myriad possible values that inform it. Sometimes starting with what you want, and then reflecting on why you want it, can help you determine what matters most.

MAKE IT SO

The next process is **Make it So**, or in ACT-speak, Committed Action. This process represents the commitment in Acceptance and Commitment Therapy, because while it's great to do the internal work that comes with the other five processes, at some point you do have to *do* something. You have to commit to taking action toward what matters most in your life.

Although there is no set order to the six core processes, Determine What Matters is an ideal prerequisite to Make it So. After all, it doesn't make much sense to take action in your life without first connecting with what's important to you. For instance, if you want to drive somewhere you've never been before, you wouldn't just get in the car and go. You'd open Waze or Google Maps or whatever GPS program you use, enter the address, and follow the directions. It's the same thing with life. When you Determine What Matters, you create your personal GPS program, and you can use it to direct any action you take. When your values inform what you do, you are far more likely to enjoy the process and to be satisfied with the results.

Make it So is a twofold process. It requires your action to be relevant to your desire (what you want) *and* to your values (why you want it). If a certain decision or action helps you achieve a goal but it's not in alignment with what matters most to you, then you probably won't feel content with your results. Sure, you've accomplished something, but it feels inconsistent with who you are and why you're here on this planet. Any happiness from achieving that goal will be short-lived.

But when you know who you are, what you want, and why you want it . . . and then you go out into the world and make it happen? That's what I call soul work, and it's what heart-centered, soul-anchored entrepreneurs do best. When you're able to merge your purpose and your passion to create something new in the world, there is nothing more beautiful, powerful, and exciting than that.

CREATE SPACE

Another core process of psychological flexibility is **Create Space**, or in ACT terminology, Cognitive Defusion. This process gives us the power to create distance from our thoughts, so that they don't overly influence our feelings and our behaviors. Instead, we allow thoughts to come and go as they please without trying to stop, control, or avoid them.

The word *fusion* means "the process or result of joining two or more things together to form a single entity," according to the *Oxford*

Dictionary. In the world of ACT, we use the word *fusion* to describe the joining of our thoughts with our identity, which then gives our thoughts a lot of control our behavior. Here's another entirely hypothetical example that has never happened to me before (#sarcasm):

> *While getting dressed, I look in the mirror and think to myself,* Ugh, I'm fat. *I proceed to berate myself with a litany of judgments and negative self-talk:* Of course you're fat. You eat way too much processed foods and sugar. You have zero willpower when it comes to food. And that's your problem: You're weak. Look at all of these other people who manage to stay thin. What's wrong with you? *I throw on a baggy pair of yoga pants and head to my kitchen, where I proceed to comfort myself with dark chocolate and potato chips.*

In this example, I have accepted the assumptions that 1) being "fat" is a bad thing, and 2) I am fat and therefore I am bad. I bought into the thought and it became a part of my identity. I've fused myself with the thought and I believe I'm fat. The thought *I'm fat* influences my behaviors as I descend into a shame spiral and turn to emotional eating.

So what's the alternative? We can notice the thought and Create Space for it. Let's replay this scenario, but this time, we'll apply this process:

> *While getting dressed, I look in the mirror and think to myself,* Ugh, I'm fat. *I stop and notice the thought:* Oh, look. I'm having the thought that I'm fat. *I pause for a moment and acknowledge the feelings of frustration and sadness that come up, and I ask myself how helpful the thought is. It carries a lot of judgment and doesn't make me feel good about myself or others. But it also points out that maybe I'm not paying as much attention to my nutrition and physical activity as I'd like to, especially because it's important to me to be healthy. As I continue to get dressed, I decide to look up some healthy recipes and take a walk after work.*

In that second example, I've stopped the shame spiral in its tracks. First, I acknowledge the thought (and the emotions that come with it; more on that in the next section) without judgment. Second, I ask an important question: How helpful is this thought? Once I work through those two questions, I then identify what matters to me (my value of health) and what I want to do about it (find healthy recipes and go for a walk). I'm pulling in the processes of Determine What Matters and Make it So.

The process of Create Space is essentially that first step: When you notice the thought, you're looking *at* your thoughts rather than *from* your thoughts. The second step is how you respond once you are aware of the thought, which focuses on workability rather than fact. It honestly doesn't matter whether or not the thought is true. What matters most is whether it helps you take action that's consistent with who you are and what you want.

Sometimes it's not necessary to ask yourself the workability question, particularly if it's not an emotionally charged thought. Sometimes, we simply notice our thoughts and create thought space, allow them to continue, and then return to what we were doing.

LET IT BE

I call the next core process **Let it Be**, which in ACT terminology is Acceptance. As its name suggests, acceptance is a key component of both Acceptance and Commitment Therapy and psychological flexibility. Where Create Space is about your thoughts, Let it Be is about your feelings. It's about making space for all of your emotions, sensations, cravings, urges, and desires, no matter how painful they are. Instead of trying to avoid, resist, or get rid of them, you simply allow them to be. Just as you notice a thought, you notice a feeling and let it in.

Rather than call these feelings "bad" or even "unpleasant," I choose to refer to them as "unwanted." Doing so strips them of any judgment or implication that we're not supposed to feel them, and instead frames them simply as feelings we don't want to have.

Frequently, when we experience an unwanted emotion, we label it as "bad" or "wrong" and proceed to try to ignore, minimize, or dodge it. This is often a lesson we learn at a very young age. A well-intentioned adult may comfort us when we're hurt by telling us, "Don't cry"; or perhaps a less-well-intentioned adult may threaten us when we're upset, telling us, "Stop crying, or I'll give you something to cry about." The truth is, in both of these situations the intention is irrelevant. The underlying message is "It's not okay to feel what you feel, so stop feeling it."

It's not just sadness or tears that elicit this response from people. All sorts of emotions can be considered taboo, including anger, depression, anxiety, rage, loneliness—the list goes on, and is reflected in common phrases like *Boys don't cry, Good girls don't get mad, Snap out of it, Calm down,* and so forth. These messages are rarely helpful (when was the last time you felt more relaxed when someone told you to calm down?), and yet we internalize them so that they become second nature.

Because we believe we're not supposed to have these feelings, we do our best to get rid of them. We mask our sadness with a smile and tell everyone we're doing fine when we're not. We have one too many drinks to dull the edge of social anxiety. We stuff down our anger, only to have it emerge later at an unsuspecting target. Our efforts to avoid unwanted feelings usually result in unwanted behaviors, which heightens our shame and increases our sense of disconnection and dissatisfaction.

The antidote is to accept the feeling, or let the emotion be. This sounds simple, and it is. But that doesn't mean it's easy. For most people, the thought of creating space and allowing an unwanted feeling is terrifying, and it's so much easier to return to our default setting of avoid, block, resist. But the truth is, you cannot outrun your feelings. Eventually, they catch up to you, and when they do, the consequences are even worse.

Let it Be is an active process that requires a willingness to face difficult emotions head-on. It's a common misconception that acceptance means just letting things happen, and that's not at all what I advocate. It's not passively rolling over and allowing life to happen to you. It's understanding that you will have these emotions whether you want them or not, so you're not going to waste time and energy fighting against them. Instead, you breathe into them, let them be, and re-anchor yourself in what matters most so that you can keep moving forward. In this way, it complements the process of Create Space, and allows us to reconnect with Determine What Matters and Make it So. (See how all these processes start to work together? And we still have two more to go!)

ANCHOR YOURSELF

The next core process is **Anchor Yourself**, or in ACT language, Contact with the Present Moment. When you Anchor Yourself, you are fully present, connected, and engaged with whatever is happening in the present moment. At first glance, this looks like it would be a simple process to master: just say focused on the present moment. And, as with all of the processes, it is simple—and not easy.

Your mind is an incredible machine that constantly processes sensory information, makes judgments, reviews the past, and plans your next move. While this is helpful from an evolutionary perspective (it's the reason our species survived!), it makes it much more difficult to stay grounded in the present. If you've ever practiced mindfulness meditation, you know how just how difficult it can be to stay anchored in the now. You close your eyes, you notice your breath . . . and then your mind drifts, replaying events from the past or making plans about the future.

It's so easy to get distracted by these thoughts or carried away by feelings of anxiety, fear, anger, and doubt. When you do so, you disconnect from the world around you—from whom you're with, what you're doing, and why you're doing it. Maybe you even get so distracted that you go full autopilot and completely lose track of yourself in the world. (If you've ever gotten home and realized you have no recollection of the walk or drive there, you know what I'm talking about.)

But when we practice anchoring ourselves, we retrain our minds to remain focused on the present moment. You can focus on the external physical world, your internal psychological world, or both at the same time. And when your attention slips, you simply acknowledge that your thoughts or emotions distracted you and immediately return your attention to the present moment.

This process works in tandem with the other four processes I've already described and heightens their effectiveness. When you Anchor Yourself, you remain connected with what matters most, and you're able to act on what matters to you with purpose and intention. When your thoughts or feelings pull you away from the present, you can Create Space or Let it Be, and return your attention to the present moment so that you can continue to do what matters.

OBSERVE YOURSELF

The final process of psychological flexibility is **Observe Yourself**, or in true ACT jargon, Self-as-Context. Here's the point in the book where we get a little meta, so get ready to have your mind blown. Actually, get ready to get both parts of your mind blown.

When we talk about the mind, we usually think of the internal monologue that's constantly running in our head. This is the "Thinking Self," and it is always working to create thoughts, memories, beliefs, ideas, plans, dreams, and so forth. It's your inner voice, the one that's constantly perceiving and judging all of the information you're processing, and it's the subject when you Create Space or Anchor Yourself.

But there's another part to your mind that may be new to you, and this is the "Observer Self." This is the part of you that's always aware of what you're thinking, feeling, sensing, or doing. In ACT this is also referred to as "pure awareness," because you are fully aware of your life experience as you're having it.

This can be a little difficult to explain with words, so let's do a quick exercise instead:

1. First, imagine yourself at age 7. Remember what you looked

like, the thoughts you had, the feelings you felt, and what you liked to do; really immerse yourself in your 7-year-old self.

2. Next, remember yourself when you were 17, and all the thoughts, feelings, and experiences you had at that age.

3. Finally, connect with yourself at your current age, whatever that may be. Reflect on what it feels like to live your life today.

If you're like most people, the thoughts, feelings, and actions you experienced at age 7 probably changed when you were 17. And they probably changed again from when you were 17 to today.

So the you who thought, felt, and experienced those things—the Thinking Self —changed. But the "you" who observed those things remained the same. There's a part of you that remains constant throughout your life, always observing, always aware. She's always been with you, and she will continue to be present for the rest of your life. This is the Observer Self.

Human beings are unique in that we can create, live out, and observe an experience all at once. As I type this paragraph, I am fully aware that I am typing this paragraph. My Thinking Self is deciding which words to use, creating the sentences, and judging what I write as good or bad. At the same time, my Observer Self is noticing that I'm having these thoughts. Where the Thinking Self does all the talking, the Observer Self does all the noticing. The Thinking Self may change over time, but the Observer Self is constant.

I warned you this was meta! But I promise it's not meta just for the sake of being meta. It's a key component of psychological flexibility for a reason. When you adopt the viewpoint of the Observer Self, you can notice your thoughts, feelings, and memories with a sense of freedom. You don't get caught up in the chatter of the Thinking Self because you understand it's temporary and transient. Instead, you Anchor Yourself, and are able to Determine What Matters and Make it So. And when you get pulled away by the Thinking Self, you can Create Space and Let it Be, thereby returning to the moment with full awareness.

BRINGING IT ALL TOGETHER

Whew! We just covered a lot! If this were a football game, it would be the perfect time for the halftime show, or at least an extended commercial break. So if you need a breather, take one. Refill whatever you're drinking, grab a snack, maybe even take a quick walk. And when you're ready, come back and we'll do a quick review.

Ready? Excellent.

So far, you've learned to think of your mind as something separate from yourself. You have a thorough understanding of meaning, mindset, and mindfulness, and you also understand how they work together to create flexibility in our thinking and approach to life. You know a little bit more about Acceptance and Commitment Therapy and its core concept of psychological flexibility, and you see how relevant it is to small business owners and entrepreneurs. Finally, you know the basics about the six core processes, which build your flexibility, your resilience, and your overall satisfaction with life.

My hope is that you see how each of these topics work together and build upon each other. You're weaving a gorgeous tapestry, with each idea being a strand that connects with the others, creating your ideal image of your business and your life. To help explain how the six core processes work together, I think of them in terms of the six journalistic questions: who, what, where, when, why, and how. All six questions are needed to tell a good story, just as all six processes are needed for full flexibility.

- **WHO—Observe Yourself.** *Who* are you? You are two elements: the Thinking Self and the Observer Self.
- **WHAT—Create Space.** *What* you think doesn't define who you are.
- **WHERE—Let it Be.** By no longer escaping from your emotions, you are here, *where* you belong.
- **WHEN—Anchor Yourself.** The present moment is the only *when* that matters.
- **WHY—Determine What Matters.** *Why* are your values important to you?

- **HOW—Make it So.** *How* will you translate your values into action?

Each process builds upon and strengthens the others, so remember: There's no single correct way or order to practice or implement them. Some people like to start with an action-oriented approach (Determine What Matters and Make it So), which flows into the more internal work of the other four processes. Other people prefer to take an inside-out approach, starting with the inner workings of the mind (Create Space and Let it Be), then moving into the present moment (Anchor Yourself and Observe Yourself), and finally moving to action (Determine What Matters and Make it So).

For the purpose of this book, I'm going to start with action and then discuss the internal processes. But first, we need to talk about the "flip side" of each of the six processes. I call them the shadow processes, and they are the reason we struggle, suffer, and stagnate in our businesses and our lives.

CHAPTER 5

The Six Shadow Processes

EACH OF THE SIX CORE PROCESSES has a corresponding process that promotes psychological inflexibility. In ACT, these are referred to as the six core pathological processes—and to be honest with you, I hate that term. I recoil at the word *pathological*. Literally, I physically cringe every time I hear it, because it carries such strong negative connotations. It's an example of the traditional medical model at work, conjuring up the idea that there's something wrong with or broken in a person, requiring a fix.

The irony is that this is exactly what an ACT-based approach seeks to change. In ACT, we are observing thoughts, feelings, and behaviors without judgment, and then choosing to respond with values-based action. We don't judge things as wrong, broken, or pathological; we're simply interested in what works and what doesn't. This is why I prefer to refer to these processes as shadow processes. There's nothing inherently bad or evil about a shadow. It's natural that everything casts a shadow when the light hits it. And when we shine the light directly on a subject, the shadows disappear. That's what the six core processes do to the six shadow processes: When we practice them, we shine a light into our darkness and the shadows disappear.

As we explore the shadow processes, I encourage you to notice what comes up for you. Being aware of how the shadow processes show up in your life is critical if you're going to overcome them. Often, these processes show up in ways we don't even recognize, at the subconscious or unconscious level. And they are the reason we don't experience the growth or success we want in our businesses and our lives. But by raising our awareness—by shining that flashlight on these processes—we bring our fears out of the shadows and into the light, where we're able to address them head-on.

As with the core processes, I have renamed the shadow processes in order to remove jargon and increase usability. Entrepreneurial flexibility requires a willingness to face these processes head-on. Are there certain shadow processes that resonate with you? Which ones show up regularly in your business, in your relationships, or generally in your life? And the most important question: How are these shadow processes working for or against your efforts? These are tough questions, but the answers will provide insight into how you're showing up in your life today and what you can do to make progress tomorrow.

The Six Core Processes of Entrepreneurial and Psychological Inflexibility	
Core Processes of Entrepreneurial Inflexibility	**Core Processes of Psychological Inflexibility**
Losing Focus	Lack of Values Clarity/Context
Sisyphus Effect	Unworkable Action
Getting Hooked	Cognitive Fusion
Running Away	Experiential Avoidance
Time Traveling	Dominance of the Conceptualized Past and Future / Limited Self Knowledge
Role Playing	Attachment to the Conceptualized Self

LOSING FOCUS

I call the shadow process of Determine What Matters **Losing Focus**, because that's how it feels when you're operating from this space. The terminology for this process in ACT is called Lack of Values Context and Clarity. Most of your day-to-day actions are in response to stress, obligations, or boredom. You're either putting out fires, doing what you have to do to get by, or zoning out. This leads to feeling disconnected from yourself and what really matters, and simply getting by in life. Without your values to guide you, you feel directionless and lost.

Here's an example of Losing Focus in action:

> *I wake to the sound of my alarm and immediately slam the snooze button. The thought of getting up makes me want to pull the covers over my head and never leave my bed. Then I remember I have a major project due tomorrow, and if I don't get it done, my client is going to be furious. I force myself to rise, grab a cup of coffee, and sit down at my computer to read the dozens of new emails that came in overnight. I check Facebook and catch up on my friends' lives, and before I know it, an hour has passed and I'm still in my pajamas. I open my client's file and stare at a blank page in front of me, completely uninspired and unsure how I'm going to get this project done in time. I think to myself,* Maybe I'm just not cut out for this.

Whew! Can you feel the draining, destructive energy in this hypo-thetical-yet-all-too-real scenario? I got sad just writing it! But most of us have felt this before, and perhaps you're feeling it now. If so, take a deep breath, exhale slowly, and remind yourself that it won't always be this way. There are options, and in fact, that's what this book is all about.

In this scenario, we're dealing with two issues: fear and avoidance. These two blocks have a lot to do with another shadow process, but I bring them up now because they tend to show up when we're out of sync with what matters to us. When you're uncertain of or dis-connected from your values, your life can seem drab and routine, and you become an automaton going through the motions. That is, until a crisis comes up, and then you respond with anxious urgency in order to fix what's wrong. Your stress levels rise, then you come crashing down, even more unsatisfied than you were before.

Getting back in touch with what's important is the antidote to feeling Losing Focus. When you have clarity about your core beliefs and values, you raise your awareness and expand your options. You can anchor your actions in what matters most to you, allowing you to find meaning in even mundane or unwanted tasks.

SISYPHUS EFFECT

The shadow process of Make it So is something I refer to as the **Sisyphus Effect** (or in ACT language, Unworkable Action). You may remember Sisyphus from sixth-grade Greek mythology, so apologies if this triggers any horrible middle school memories. Sisyphus was a narcissistic and traitorous king who was doomed to a terrible fate in the Underworld. He was forced to roll a boulder up a hill, only to have it roll back down once he neared the top, a task he would repeat for eternity. Today, the Sisyphus Effect describes repetitive, arduous behaviors that don't advance you toward your goal.

The Sisyphus Effect also appears in the world of physics, specifically low-temperature physics. It involves using lasers to hit atoms at different angles, which cools and traps them, forcing them to "roll down" a hill of potential energy until they lose all of their kinetic energy. I love this concept, because it is a perfect metaphor for what happens when your actions are disconnected from what matters to you: You expend a lot of energy trying to get things done, but ultimately trap yourself in a pattern that prevents you from getting what you really want.

Any time you engage in behavior that distances you from your values and your core identity, you are getting caught up in the Sisyphus Effect. These actions impede your ability to create successful businesses and fulfilling lives, and instead trap you in a cycle of "struggle and stuck," in which you resist your soul's calling, experience the pain of doing so, and wind up feeling anxious, frustrated, and paralyzed.

There are two types of behavior that can get you caught in the Sisyphus Effect. The first is when you react automatically rather than respond intentionally. In this case, your behavior is usually defensive, impulsive, or reflexive, and you don't feel totally in control of your actions. If you've ever felt triggered by something or someone and had an immediate behavioral response that didn't feel great, you've experienced the Sisyphus Effect.

The second type is slightly subtler but just as insidious. Rather than react to what triggers you, you choose behaviors that allow you to ignore or resist it. It tends to show up as procrastination, avoidance, or resistance, and can include putting off work, emotional eating, not hanging out with friends or family, misusing drugs or alcohol, binging on television or social media—you get the idea. Any behavior that pulls you further into the morass of confusion and disconnection is the Sisyphus Effect in action. No matter how much you engage in these behaviors, they won't get you closer to your goal, and the boulder rolls downhill again.

The answer to the Sisyphus Effect is to Make it So—to take action that is consistent with your values and what matters most in your life. This involves responding intentionally rather than reacting automatically and taking proactive behavior. In Chapter 8, I'll provide you with some tools and strategies that can help you overcome the initial inertia of the Sisyphus Effect, so that you can get back to work on the life you want.

GETTING HOOKED

The shadow process of Create Space is **Getting Hooked**, and in ACT parlance, this is called Cognitive Fusion. When you experience Getting Hooked, you are your thoughts, plain and simple. You don't see yourself as separate from the messages your mind feeds you, and you're so caught up in your thoughts that they dictate your behavior. There isn't much insight or awareness going on when you're submitting to your thoughts, which makes it much more likely that you'll feel Losing Focus and experience the Sisyphus Effect.

Think of it this way: Have you ever had a close friend go emotionally MIA on you when she starts dating someone new? You still hang out with her, but everything is now 100% defined by her relationship to her partner. It's all "Kevin and I loved that movie!" or "Kelsey and I don't like Chinese food." She is totally subsumed by the relationship, and it's hard to know where she stands, other than with her new squeeze. You're left wondering what happened to your friend, and who this new person is who no longer goes with you for dim sum on Saturday afternoons.

Essentially, this is what happens when you experience Getting Hooked, because you no longer define yourself separately from your thoughts. Your thoughts are the Kevin/Kelsey in your relationship with your mind—joined at the hip, completely inseparable, and probably not in a totally healthy way. Your mind may be feeding you unhelpful or destructive thoughts, which might make you feel anxious, sad, frustrated, and helpless. But you submit to your thoughts and believe them wholeheartedly, because you are fused with them (hence the ACT term *fusion*) and don't see another way out.

Those unwanted feelings of frustration and sadness create an undercurrent of tension because you know this isn't right. You sense that you don't have to feel this way, and you may not like or even believe the thoughts your mind is feeding you. But the problem is, when you're in the throes of Getting Hooked, you don't realize there's another way.

The good news is that there is another approach: to Create Space. Whereas in Getting Hooked you believe a thought is absolutely true, when you Create Space you realize it may or may not be. Instead of viewing the thought as threatening or problematic you see it for what it is—just words, which carry no true threat. Even though the thought may feel real, it's not. It's just words or images that your mind created, and it has little or nothing to do with what's happening in the world around you. Kevin/Kelsey doesn't get to determine its importance. You do. And you get to decide how much attention you give it.

RUNNING AWAY

The opposing process to Let it Be is what I call **Running Away**, and it's what ACT practitioners call Experiential Avoidance. This happens when you attempt to avoid, remove, ignore, or escape from what ACT practitioners call unwanted "private experiences." These private experiences include thoughts, feelings, memories, images, urges, and sensations—things that you know you're experiencing but no one else would just by looking at you. By running from these experiences, you are running away from yourself and your truth.

In ACT, we talk a lot about the mind being an incredible problem-solver. Your mind is able to figure out what to do to fix any sort of obstacle, stumbling block, or big issue that you're confronted with, and this is particularly helpful for external problems. For example, if you're driving down the road and see a pothole, your mind starts problem-solving: It tells you to drive around it, so that you don't ruin your car's alignment and cause hundreds of dollars' worth of damage. In this case, problem-solving is really helpful, and the idea of avoiding the pothole is the right strategy. It's going to cause pain or problems, so you simply go around it.

But here's the thing: Problem-solving doesn't always work with those pesky private experiences I mentioned earlier, and the mind doesn't readily distinguish between external and internal experiences. It wants to respond to sadness the same way it responds to a pothole; sadness causes damage and pain, which is no good, so let's go around it. That's why our default response is often to avoid, block, repress, or ignore those feelings we don't want.

Part of the problem stems from the tendency to judge thoughts, feelings, and memories. We think of them as good or bad, right or wrong, pleasant or painful, and when you judge them this way, the mind responds accordingly. "Good" thoughts and feelings are safe; "bad" thoughts and feelings are a problem. So when you have a "bad" feeling, your mind views it as a problem and kicks into action. It is going to solve the problem by trying to run away from it.

Often, we run away by distracting ourselves from that unwanted experience. Television, social media, work, food, sex, and drugs are all great distractions from your inner pain. It goes without saying that drug and alcohol abuse can exacerbate our problems, and using them to distract from unwanted emotions is abusive. You can only outrun your emotions for so long; they will always catch up with you.

But even excessive amounts of "good" things can be problematic, and it gets a little tricky when we start talking about coping mechanisms. On the surface, coping strategies appear to be a healthy alternative to experiencing feelings we don't want. Going for a run, checking in with a friend, reading a book—all of these may be enjoyable and even healthy activities, and I don't discourage them. But if you use those activities to distract yourself from your underlying emotions, you're not doing yourself any favors. It's just another way of avoiding how you really feel, and that's not going to work out well in the long run.

So instead of running away from your feelings, maybe you decide to tolerate them. You grit your teeth and bear a miserable experience; you muscle through and make the best of a bad situation. On the surface, this might look like acceptance, or letting your emotions be. It's not. There's a huge difference between tolerating something and accepting it, and that has to do with willingness. When you tolerate something, you're still judging it as "bad" or something you don't want but have anyway. When you accept something, you remove judgment from the picture and you view it more objectively.

That's why the first step toward changing how you respond to unwanted feelings is to Let it Be, or to practice acceptance. By doing so, you retrain the mind to view those private experiences differently. You no longer have to view them as problems that need to be solved. Instead, you see them as just one aspect of your experience, and not something to get rid of. Let it Be is about approaching your feelings from a place of non-judgment, so that you don't get caught up in the emotions and allow them to drive your behavior.

TIME TRAVELING

The shadow process of Anchor Yourself is what I call **Time Traveling**, or in ACT terminology (and get ready for a mouthful), Dominance of the Conceptualized Past and Future/Limited Self

Knowledge—which basically means you're either living in the past or living in the future, and that results in feeling out of touch with yourself.

Together, Getting Hooked and Running Away are responsible for almost all internal conflict. Either we're so attached to our thoughts and feelings that they dictate our identity and behaviors, or we're trying to avoid them so that we don't have to deal with them. The end result of both processes is the same: We feel disconnected from our true self, overwhelmed by our private experiences (no matter how much we don't want to be), and disengaged from the present moment.

When you get caught up in your thoughts and feelings, it's often about something that has already happened (leading you to ruminate about the past) or something that is yet to happen (so you're fretting about the future). In either case, you're immediately pulled out of the present moment and no longer fully aware of what's happening in the world in front of you.

Vulnerability moment: This happens to me *all the time*. If I have a conversation with someone that doesn't go well, I replay it in my head over and over. I come up with the perfect thing I should have said (after the fact, of course), and I berate myself by recalling everything that I did wrong. Or, if I know I have to have an uncomfortable conversation with someone, my mind creates a fantasy version of what will happen, and it's easy for me to get preemptively angry or upset as a result. That's right: I get angry about something that hasn't even happened yet. Talk about "limited self-knowledge." (Insert eye roll here.)

This is how Time Traveling goes hand-in-hand with Getting Hooked and Running Away. When you overidentify with your thoughts, feelings, and memories, it's easy to get stuck in the past or flipped into the future. Those unwanted private experiences run roughshod over your present moment experience, causing you to feel out of control and disconnected from who you are, what you're doing, and what matters most to you.

That's why the Anchor Yourself process is so effective in responding to the distress that comes from Time Traveling. It's a gentle reminder that we only have this moment, and we miss out on life if we're constantly consumed by the past or the future. To quote philosopher Alan Watts, "I have realized that the past and future are real illusions, that they exist in the present, which is what there is and all there is."

Side note: Time Traveling isn't limited to unwanted thoughts and feelings. It's just as possible to get caught up in a happy memory or in anticipation of a future event. This isn't necessarily a bad thing, and it can feel rewarding to remember something pleasant or exciting to look forward to something fun. Just make sure you approach it mindfully and intentionally, so that you're finding balance between the past, future, and present. If the paths of nostalgia and anticipation lead you too far astray, they dull the beauty of where you are now.

ROLE PLAYING

The shadow process of Observe Yourself is what I call **Role Playing**, also called Attachment to the Conceptualized Self or Self-as-Content in ACT language. When you engage in Role Playing, you unconsciously define yourself according to how your Thinking Self views you. Your perception of yourself is limited to certain aspects of your identity, and you're not in touch with the Observer Self, the constant presence that's with you throughout your life.

Each one of us has an image of ourselves that tells a story about who we are in the world. As an example, I'll share some aspects of my story with you. There are demographic components: I'm a woman, I'm white, I'm married, I'm American. There are also the different parts I play: I'm a coach, a therapist, a wife, a mother, a daughter, a sister, a small business owner, a friend. Then add in my strengths and weaknesses: I'm intelligent, I'm intuitive, I'm methodical, I'm overly emotional, I'm not good at sports, I'm a procrastinator. On top of that, add in my likes and dislikes, my vision and goals, my relationships, and you can see that I'm a complex, multifaceted human being. Just like you.

Now, there's nothing inherently wrong with allowing my story to inform my self-perception and my decisions. However, if I get so caught up in the story of myself that I can't see past it—I'm *only* what my story tells me I am—then that can be problematic. By playing the role the story sets for me, I limit my options and can get stuck.

Let's say, hypothetically speaking of course, that I want to write a book. If I'm immersed in my story, I might think, *I'm such a procrastinator; I'll never get it done.* In this case, I'm allowing one part of my story (I am a procrastinator) to influence how I think and feel about what I want. A more positive aspect of my story might even sneak in there and bully me a bit: *Why am I procrastinating so much? I'm smart enough to know better!* Now I'm super-fused with a story that's feeding me unhelpful thoughts and feelings, and I'm playing the role of the Smart Person who Can't Finish Her Shit. How likely is it that my behaviors will fall in line with my role? Yeah, it's practically guaranteed.

***

All of the six core processes can work together to break this cycle, but it starts with Observe Yourself. First and foremost, I need to recognize that while I *have* a story that informs who I am and what I do, I *am not* the story. There is a part of me that remains outside the story—the Observer Self—which means I'm not limited by the roles I play. From there, I can pull in the other five processes to help me connect with the present moment and take intentional action, all while holding my story lightly and without judgment.

CHAPTER 6

The Basics of Entrepreneurial Flexibility

NOW YOU HAVE A general understanding of the six core processes (and their shadow processes) that form the basis of Acceptance and Commitment Therapy. You've seen how Determine What Matters, Make it So, Create Space, Let it Be, Anchor Yourself, and Observe Yourself work together to promote psychological flexibility. The thread that weaves these processes together is your consciousness, or your awareness. That's your ability to perceive, sense, and understand the world around you and the world within you.

Traditionally, these concepts have lived primarily in the land of psychology or self-development. However, they hold great value outside the context of psychology as well, and when applied in the professional and entrepreneurial space, they will revolutionize the way we approach business and success. By expanding the basic premise of ACT and developing a model of "entrepreneurial flexibility," we can change the world.

Therefore, I'd like to propose a definition of entrepreneurial flexibility, inspired by Russ Harris and his definition of psychological flexibility:

> **Entrepreneurial flexibility (EF) is the ability to be fully present in our business, with total awareness of our self and with openness to opportunity, and to take action guided by our business principles and personal values.**

My vision is for every entrepreneur to readily access their own entrepreneurial flexibility and grow dynamic businesses that improve the world. I want every business owner to have the knowledge, ability, and confidence to utilize the six core processes, allowing them to develop a positive business mindset, strengthen business operations, and achieve success that benefits themselves and others.

Entrepreneurial flexibility is a holistic approach that creates harmony among the mind, the heart, and the spirit. When all three are in alignment, we can operate from a place that's consistent with our ethics and values, and create anything we want in business—and in life. We have the fortitude to brave the storms in our business, and the insight to navigate growth and success. Most importantly, we experience a sense of inner joy, peace, and contentment, knowing that we have everything we need to create the business and life we desire.

Now for a dose of truth: EF is not a magic pill. It's not something you achieve once and you're good to go for the rest of your life. The goal is not to sustain, or even to maintain, it. The more we try to grasp and hold tight to it, the less we have of it. Instead, EF is a process. It's a journey with no single destination because there are always new paths to explore and new experiences to enjoy.

It might be helpful to use an analogy to describe entrepreneurial flexibility. Think of EF as a muscle you can target and condition, just as you would any other muscle in your body. First, you have to engage your EF muscle, pushing ever so slightly past your comfort zone so that you have to work a bit. You complete your reps, then rest and repeat. Just as with weight training, you don't want to do too much too soon, or you run the risk of straining the muscle (or in the case of EF, burning out). But with consistent practice, you'll build strength and endurance, and your business will grow stronger too.

The rest of this book is your EF training plan. I provide you with the information, strategy, and exercises you need in order to learn the six core processes and apply them to your business. With consistent practice, you'll be amazed at the transformation you see in yourself as an entrepreneur and in your business. You'll be able to manage the day-to-day wins and losses of business ownership, as well as the major victories and defeats, with a calm confidence that stems from being fully aware of who you are, as an entrepreneur, a business owner, and a person.

But before we delve into the six processes of EF and how to apply them, let's first get clear on your vision—your ideal future for your business and your life. To do so, I want you to answer three questions:

- What do you want?
- Why do you want it?
- What stands in your way?

How you answer these questions is entirely up to you. Some people find that keeping a journal and writing down their responses works best for them. Other people are verbal processors and love to talk through these questions with someone they trust. (Bonus tip: This makes for *very* interesting date night conversation!) You might find that tapping into your creativity works well here. You can create a vision board for each question (real or virtual; Pinterest is great for that!). There's no right or wrong way to do this. The important thing is that you find what works best for you, and then do it.

WHAT DO YOU WANT?

The first step is to be clear on what it is you want. Sounds simple, right? Well, by now you know that most of what I'm talking about is simple, but not easy. The same holds true with establishing your vision. Being clear on what you want and what you're working toward is not always a straightforward process. So let's break it down a bit further.

Inevitably, when I ask a client what they want, they start broad. "I want to be happy" is a common answer, as is "I want to make more money." Sometimes "I want to feel more in control of my business" comes up too. All three of these are valid, understandable desires, and I want my clients to experience them too! But while they are a great starting point, they don't go nearly far enough in helping us create a vision of our ideal future. We've got to dig a little deeper and get at the core of what's behind the desire.

As an example, let's start with our entrepreneur who wants to "feel more in control of my business." Because honestly, whether it's revenue, expenses, staffing, product creation, or profit, I've yet to meet an entrepreneur who doesn't want to feel more in control of those things. But hidden within that desire is the truth: She doesn't feel in control of her business. In fact, it wouldn't surprise me if she feels over-whelmed, anxious, guilty, and uncertain about her business. And this probably clashes with her sense of competence and confidence about whatever service she provides or product she delivers. She's great at working *in* her business, but not so much working *on* it.

Her first step is to clearly define where she is now and what's not working. She's going to take a long, hard look at her business and articulate the issues that are causing her to feel out of control. And I'm not going to lie: Sometimes this part kind of sucks. No one likes to list all the things that aren't going right in their business or their life, and that level of honest self-reflection can sting a bit. Fortu-nately, this is one area in which the six core processes can help, because they teach us how to approach our thoughts and feelings from a place of non-judgment and curiosity, making it so much easier to take stock of what's working and what's not.

Armed with the knowledge of what's not working right, then we start creating a detailed image of the future she wants, one in which she feels in control of her business. So let's imagine that in six months, she feels a greater sense of control over her business. If I had a time machine, and she and I could jump forward six months in time, what would we see? Who are her clients? Where is she working? How does she spend a typical day? Who is a part of her business team? What strategies and processes are in place that make her feel in control? What do her financials look like? How does she feel? If we were to jump forward one year, three years, or five years in the future, what else would we see?

You can see how important it is to ask very specific questions in order to create a clear picture of the future you want. And because you're using your imagination, there are no right or wrong answers, and nothing is off-limits. This is your time to be as bold and wild as you want, to throw everything at the wall and see what sticks. This is *your* vision; it's *your* future. It can be whatever you want it to be.

So now we have a clear idea of the future, and we're good to go, right? Not so fast. There are still two more questions to tackle.

WHY DO YOU WANT IT?

Once you have an idea of what you want, the next step is to articulate why you want it. What is it about your vision that is worth working for—even fighting for? What's your big why? Too many entrepreneurs skip over this part, eager to create the future they want. But without anchoring our vision to our why, we're a ship without a rudder, easily swayed by the next tide (or fad). Getting clear on your why and connecting it with your vision are critical parts of preparing for success.

A decade ago, this idea of knowing your why was still relatively new. Sure, plenty of companies had mission statements, and some even had well-articulated company values. But having a clear why was still a fairly new concept. That is, until Simon Sinek published *Start with Why* and delivered one of the most popular and most-watched TED Talks of all time.[3] His work inspired not just entrepreneurs, but people all over the world, and I credit him with a significant paradigm shift in the entrepreneurial space.

In *Start with Why* and in his TED Talk, Sinek introduces the concept of the Golden Circle, which kind of looks like a target with three zones. Sinek argues that most companies place *what* in the center. They prioritize what they do or what they produce, and so it falls in the bull's-eye. The second ring is *how*—how they go about providing their service or product. Finally, the last ring and the furthest zone is *why*, or why what they do or make is important.

However, Sinek suggests that successful, innovative companies take the reverse approach. Rather than prioritizing the *what*, they (wait for it) start with *why* and place *that* in the bull's-eye. These organizations are crystal clear on why they are in business, which informs the second ring, or *how* they serve their customers. The outer ring, or *what*, is merely a manifestation of the *why*. *What*, may be the end result, but it doesn't drive the company. It starts with *why*.

Now, I know what some of you are thinking right now: If starting with *why* is so important, then why did I ask you to clarify your version first? Isn't vision just another way of determining *what* you want? Why not follow Sinek's advice and start with *why*?

Here's why: There's one aspect in all of this that Sinek doesn't directly address in his Golden Circle. And that's *who*. Who are the people who make up the business, and who are the people the company is serving? What are their needs, their desires, and their goals? These are critical questions that need to be answered, and I think that comes before *why*.

So here's the thing: I don't think Sinek is wrong. In fact, when we look at how businesses have traditionally operated, starting with *why* is a revolutionary concept. But especially when it comes to small business owners and entrepreneurs, I believe we need to address the *who* before we get to the Golden Circle. And in this case, creating your vision is a way of getting in touch with your *who*. Who you are influences the future you want to create. When you have a solid understanding of who you are, then it is so much easier to be clear on your why, and allow that to inform how you operate your business and what specific steps you take to serve your clients or customers.

We take a very close look at the concept of *why* in Chapter 7, devoted to Determine What Matters. Our values are the very heart of our *why*, and you'll have an opportunity to explore what matters most to you through the exercises in that chapter. This will create a solid foundation upon which you can build your business, and you'll deepen your understanding of *how* you do *what* you do.

WHAT STANDS IN YOUR WAY?

Okay, so you know what you want and you know why you want it. Time to move forward toward the future of your dreams, right? Well, almost. There's one more question to answer: What's in the way? What has kept you from achieving what you want up until now? Or, put more bluntly, why haven't you done it yet?

Hard truth: This is when your beautifully crafted vision comes up against the harsh light of reality. I absolutely, 100% believe that we can create anything we want in our lives and that no dream is too small. Whatever vision you've created for yourself, I honestly believe in your ability to make it happen. But bringing your vision to life is not all hearts and rainbows and unicorns. It's not easy. If it was, you would have already done it.

The fact is, there are always obstacles to block our path and shiny objects to distract us. There are the naysayers, the doubters, the dream destroyers. The well-intentioned friend who tries to dissuade us because she cares. (Sometimes that well-intentioned friend lives in our own mind.)

When I worked for the Air Force, we talked about LIMFACs, or limiting factors. LIMFACs were the issues that could potentially keep us from achieving the mission; they were the weakest or most inefficient part of a plan, and it was critical to assess and account for them in advance. Today, I'm asking you to assess your vision's LIMFACs, because when we take stock of our reality and acknowledge the things that have held us back in the past, we're able to prepare for them in the future. That's why identifying what's in the way of your dream is so important. Instead of avoiding it or wishing that it won't happen, you're proactively preparing for it. You're creating space for it, welcoming it, and addressing it head-on. In doing so, you increase the likelihood that you will bring your vision to life.

I find it helpful to categorize these obstacles as either external or internal blocks, because each type requires different strategies for working through them. External blocks are things outside of our minds that stand in our way. This might mean not having the tools or supplies you need, or not having a sufficient support team to help you. It might be not having enough time or money to accomplish your vision, though time and money are tricky. (Sometimes they are internal blocks masquerading as external blocks, but we get to that in a minute.) In general, external blocks can be resolved through acquisition—acquisition of knowledge, of resources, of tools, and so forth.

If external blocks are a matter of skill set development, then internal blocks are a matter of mindset development. They are the messages we have internalized over time, and often we don't even recognize they're there, because they've become an ingrained part of who we are and how we view the world. The Institute of Professional Excellence in Coaching (iPEC), through which I completed my coach training, describes four main internal blocks:

- **Limiting Beliefs:** things you accept about yourself, others, or life that limit you in some way. These are general social beliefs, such as "Boys don't cry" or "You have to work hard to succeed."

- **Interpretations:** judgments or opinions you create about someone or something and believe to be true. These are the stories we tell ourselves, such as "She didn't text me back. She must be mad at me."

- **Assumptions:** expectations that because something happened before, it will happen again. An example might be "Every time I talk about money with my business partner, we get in an argument. I know when we discuss next year's budget, we're going to wind up fighting."

- **Gremlins:** your inner critical voice that tells you that you aren't good enough. The message may vary *(You're not smart/ athletic/good-looking/rich/brave/whatever enough)* but the end result is the same: You believe you're unworthy, unlovable, or in some way not enough, and that belief keeps you stuck.

Although I've listed the four blocks in order of intensity/impact from least to greatest, iPEC switched the order to create a helpful acronym to remember them: GAIL. Your GAILs are your internal blocks and your internal LIMFACs, and they are much more destructive than any external block ever could be.

In my years as a therapist and a coach, I've yet to meet anyone who hasn't struggled under the weight of their GAILs. We all have our own inner demons and experience a degree of shame or unworthiness around them. That's the great irony: We're united in our shared experience of fearing we're not enough, and yet we don't talk about it because of fear and shame.

As you read this book, my deepest desire and sincerest hope is that the six core processes will provide a path for you to face your GAILs head-on, and, in doing so, empower you to build your business and achieve your dreams. When we develop entrepreneurial flexibility, we stop shame in its tracks, we create businesses with heart and guts, and we change the world.

And it starts now.

The Core Processes

CHAPTER 7

Determine What Matters

WHAT IS DETERMINE WHAT MATTERS?

At the heart of the Determine What Matters process is getting clear on what's most important to you, and you do that by identifying your values. The word *values* has lots of different meanings and connotations, and it may be one of the most eye roll–inducing words in the history of words. Okay, that may be an overstatement, but still—the word *values* is certainly overused, so I want to offer a basic definition of values in the context of leading a fulfilling life.

Simply put, **values are how you want to live your life**. And implicit within that short statement are three important components: qualities, desire, and action. *How* describes the qualities you want to embody, *want* indicates your desire for those qualities, and *live* suggests that there is action required. All three pieces are needed for something to be a value.

I like this definition of values because it is intentionally broad. It can be applied to your entire life, or just one aspect of it. So let's start my looking at it from an entrepreneurial perspective and the values you bring to your business. If you're like most entrepreneurs, you likely appreciate the freedom that comes with owning your business.

If so, then independence is probably one of your values. You demonstrate your desire for independence through the actions you take: setting your own hours, developing your own workflow, and so forth. In doing so, you epitomize the qualities of independence: You're self-reliant, you're motivated, and so forth.

In my case, one of the reasons I became a coach was because I wanted to help other professionals build businesses that felt like a natural extension of themselves. Nothing makes me feel quite as invigorated and fulfilled as helping someone bring their soul's purpose to life within their business, so it's probably not surprising that service is one of my business values. I strive to demonstrate my commitment to service in every aspect of my business, from networking, to building relationships, to working with clients. As a result, the qualities I show in my business include deeply caring for others, being a good listener, and approaching every interaction with empathy and focus.

It's entirely possible that neither independence nor service is a value in your business. And you know what? That is totally fine. We don't all have to have the same reasons for becoming entrepreneurs, and we're allowed to have different values. There's no right or wrong when it comes to your values because they are yours. We get to choose what matters to us, and that's at the core of Determine What Matters. (Although I must admit, sometimes I don't necessarily feel like I'm choosing the value, but rather that the value is choosing me.) In fact, when we try to live our lives according to someone else's values, we're probably going to experience a shit ton of conflict.

But what if you don't know for sure what your values are? What if you're still figuring out what you want your life to be about? Guess what? That is also totally fine. Determine What Matters is a process, and it can take time to get clear on what's important. It's also possible that your values may shift over time. My values now, as a wife and mother who is fast approaching 40, are different than they were when I was 24 and child-free, and they'll probably change again when I'm empty nesting in my 50s.

That's why it's important to remember that values are very much about *now*. They both influence and are influenced by the present moment and our current situation. If you aren't sure exactly what matters most to you, then you'll find the exercises at the end of this chapter particularly helpful. But even if you are sure, I encourage you to choose one or two of the activities and try them out. (You might surprise yourself.)

When you're not aware of what matters most to you, then you become susceptible to the shadow process: Losing Focus. While you're still able to accomplish day-to-day responsibilities, there's a sense that you're lacking fulfillment and purpose. This might make you feel anxious, uncertain, out of sync, or disconnected from yourself and your life, which can decrease your desire and motivation to make change in your life and keep you stuck. It's not pleasant to feel unmoored and unsure of yourself, but it doesn't have to become your default zone. You can get back in sync with yourself and your life by clarifying what's important to you—your values.

So to sum up what values are: They are personal, they are judgment-neutral, and they are about how you want to live today. But there are also a few things values are not. First, values are not goals. Goals are usually time-limited tasks that can be achieved, and they are future-oriented. Climbing Mount Everest is a goal. Making your first million dollars is a goal. Having a baby is a goal. But they aren't values, because values are about now and don't have a final destination. These goals may indicate underlying values, such as adventure, security, or love. And when we link our goals with our values, we're much more likely to enjoy the process of working toward them. If the goal is the destination on a map, the value is the direction you're moving. That differentiation is important.

Next, values are not feelings. Our values may influence our emotional response to a situation and our subsequent behavior, but they are not emotions themselves. Values are also not things that we can get from someone else. As I mentioned, values are personal; they are internal. The minute we start looking outside of ourselves for something, we leave the realm of personal. Respect can be a value, and you can live out that value by how you treat others. But you can't necessarily control how others treat you, so wanting or demanding respect from others is not a value.

Finally, values are not morals or ethics. This can be a little tricky, because a lot of people equate values with morals, and they are very different. Morals are about a person's beliefs regarding what is acceptable behavior, whereas values are about a person's beliefs regarding what's important to them. When I was a teenager, "family values" was a major talking point for both political parties, but really, they were talking about morals. There was a lot of judgment and condescension that accompanied "family values," so it's not surprising that many people have a difficult time viewing values as judgment-neutral.

But while morals and ethics are about *acceptable* behavior, values are about what's important to someone, and that transcends acceptability. For example, if I ask 10 people, "On a scale of 1 to 10, how important is adventure in your life?" I will likely get a range of answers. One person may rate it a 9, another a 6, another a 2, and so on. For the person who rated it a 2, it's not that adventure is a bad thing, it's just not a high priority for them. Likewise, when we look at the person who rated it a 9, it's not that adventure is inherently good, it's just that it's really important to them. So remember: The minute we find ourselves looking through a lens of right or wrong, we're no longer talking about values, but morals.

WHY IS DETERMINE WHAT MATTERS IMPORTANT?

Now that you know what values are (and what they aren't), I want you to know just why they're so important, and why Determine What Matters should be high on an entrepreneur's to-do list. In fact, the reason it's important has a lot to do with that to-do list, because once we're able to articulate our core values and guiding principles, it makes decision-making easier and task completion more enjoyable.

When I work with my private coaching clients, the first thing I want to learn is what matters most in their lives. Knowing my clients' guiding principles ensures that everything we do is congruent with what drives them. If I'm helping my client create an action plan for her business that has nothing to do with what's important to her, then she's going to have a hard time getting motivated and sticking with the plan. But when we're clear on what matters and allow our values to inspire action, then we're far more likely to be invested in the work and satisfied with the outcome.

For example, one of my clients—let's call her Jill—reported that she had been procrastinating on a major project for a client. She knew she could do the job, but she felt completely unmotivated to get started. As we dug a little deeper, Jill realized that her personal values clashed with her client's values. To be clear, there was nothing inherently bad about or wrong with either her or her client's values; after all, values are neutral. But the mismatch created a situation in which Jill dreaded completing the work, so she would procrastinate and then feel guilty and frustrated. She initially accepted the job because she was a new business owner and appreciated the stability (oh look—another value!) that income provided. So not only did Jill's values clash with the client's, but she also had an internal value clash of authenticity versus stability. Once all of that became clear, we were then able to use some of the techniques from later in this chapter to help her gain clarity and choose her next action.

In my work with entrepreneurs and small business owners like Jill, I've discovered that Determine What Matters is a useful process in general, but it's particularly helpful in five key areas: Connecting with Why, Making Decisions, Finding Your Krewe, Facing Your Fears, and Going through Hell. Let's take a look at each of these areas.

Connecting with Why

If your ultimate goal is to lead a rich, rewarding, purposeful life, then it's vital to connect what you do with why you do it. You're trying to manage the day-to-day operations as well as the long-term strategy for your company, and if you're a solopreneur, you're doing it all by yourself. You're responsible for marketing, networking, sales service delivery, product creation and inventory, project management, paying bills, taxes. That's not everything, and it's already enough to make your head spin—which is exactly why you have to be clear on why you're doing this in the first place.

Connecting with your big why keeps you fully present and engaged, and prevents you from going on autopilot. As an entrepreneur, it's easy to get caught up with (and overwhelmed by) the "must-do" items on your list. That sense of pressure and obligation can be a real joy killer, which can lead to fatigue and burnout. But by connecting even the most minor task to your business values, then you're more likely to enjoy your work, and less likely to experience burnout and boredom.

These "must do" tasks are different for everyone. For me, it's anything related to taxes (which is a bit ironic, because my mother is an accountant. Sorry, Mom.). I'm cool with doing my regular monthly bookkeeping and financial reports, but when tax season comes, my eyes glaze over. Pulling together an alphabet soup of forms—W-2s, W-4s, 1099-MISCs, and so forth—and getting everything organized so that then I can sit down and spend hours on my taxes is something I dread every year. Seriously, I hate it.

In years past, I used to procrastinate like crazy on my taxes. I would literally deep-clean my refrigerator just to avoid having to work on my taxes. Having a sparkling kitchen was nice, but it only served to increase my annoyance and anxiety about sitting down and doing my damn taxes.

Then one year, I decided it was going to be different—that *I* was going to be different. Instead of complaining, procrastinating, and dreading tax season, I was going to be proactive and get it done early. I scheduled time on my calendar to do the work, and guess what happened when that day arrived? Yep, I went straight into my kitchen and cleaned out my junk drawer.

But during my sudden onset cleaning spree, I had a conversation with myself that went a little something like this:

Inner Voice: What's going on? Why aren't you doing your taxes?

Me: Because I don't want to. It's boring and annoying and no fun.

IV: OK, so don't do them.

Me: Are you serious? I can't do that!

IV: Why not? What would happen?

Me: Um, I'd get in trouble with the IRS, probably owe more money, and it would negatively affect my business.

IV: And then what?

Me: Well, I don't know. I mean, worst-case scenario, I'd go out of business.

IV: And that would suck.

Me: Yeah, it would. Because I love my business, I love serving other people, and I love the feeling that what I do matters and that I'm empowering people to change their lives.

IV: Right. So doing your taxes actually helps you serve others and change lives.

Me: [silence]

IV: See what I mean?

Me: I hate it when you're right.

As soon as I made the connection between my business values (service and empowerment) and doing my taxes, I was not only motivated to get it done, but it felt less anxiety-provoking. Doing my taxes no longer felt like an annoying chore once it became a values-consistent action. Now, any time I'm procrastinating on something (including, ahem, writing a book) and need a boost of motivation, I connect the task with a value. Once I view it in those terms, I can't not do it.

Making Decisions

Among the alluring aspects of the entrepreneurial lifestyle are the freedom and flexibility that come with being your own boss. You don't have to get permission from anyone before making decisions for your business, and you can choose any path you want to create the business and life you want. The buck stops with you, friend. You get the final say.

Sounds amazing, right? Yeah, it totally is! Well, usually. Except for those times when you're not sure what to do. When there are two (or more) great options to choose from—or worse, when there are two (or more) terrible options to choose from—and you've got to make a decision. Then entrepreneurship can feel confusing and frustrating, especially when analysis paralysis sets in and you spend so much time (over)thinking that you get yourself stuck and have no idea what to do. Yeah, that part? Not so much fun.

That's when you can use Determine What Matters to help you, because when you're clear on what's important to you and your business, your values can guide your decision-making process. For example, if your touchstone value is service, then you can view your decisions and their impact through the lens of service. Ask yourself how each option serves your clients, your company, and your stakeholders (including yourself), and choose the one that best reflects your value of service.

Sometimes, making a decision will be that simple: identify your value and pick the option that best embodies it. Boom—done. But in the real world, it's often not that easy, and it's usually because of one of two reasons: either you have multiple options that are all in alignment with your values, or you have values that are conflicting or competing with each other. In the case of the first reason, hurray! You have some fantastic options in front of you, all of which could work. Check in with your mind, your heart, and your gut, and go with the one that feels right. You got this.

But let's be honest: A plethora of great options is usually not what makes decision-making so difficult. More likely, you have multiple values at play and you're having difficulty navigating between them. That's what I call a good old-fashioned value clash, gumming up the gears and grinding things to a halt. When this happens, the next step is to prioritize your values based on your current circumstances, and make the decision based on your priorities. This process is not only useful within your business, but when your business needs are competing with your personal life. As an entrepreneur who is also a wife and mother, this is a technique I use often. In fact, I used it this morning.

Several weeks ago, I scheduled an early-morning session with a client, and then a few days later I learned that my oldest son's class was presenting to the whole school at the start of the day. There was no way I could do both, and I was torn between my values of service and family. So I paused and evaluated the circumstances. On the work front, I knew my client was heading out of town and wanted to meet with me before leaving. When I checked in with my son, he said it would be great if I could come, but there'd be another presentation next quarter. Armed with that knowledge, I decided to keep the appointment with my client and committed to attending my son's presentation next quarter.

Admittedly, this situation seems pretty cut-and-dried, and I was fortunate that my attendance wasn't a big deal for my oldest son. It's not always this easy, and in fact, when I had to make a similar choice but involving my youngest son, it *did* matter to him and he was upset with me. Sometimes there is no easy right answer, and sometimes we don't have all of the information we need to make a decision. Even when we make choices that are informed by our values, we still may have to deal with unintended consequences or unhappy outcomes.

In the case of my oldest son, while this process helped me make a rational decision, it didn't eliminate my feelings of mom guilt—and it's not going to. It's understandable that I'd feel guilty and a little sad that most of the other kids had a parent in the audience that morning and my son didn't. Granted, he doesn't appear to be scarred for life, so I think we'll be fine in the long run—but still: My decision had emotional consequences, even though it was guided by my values. And I suspect I would have had similar feelings had I cancelled on my client. When we experience a value clash, we're going to have some unwanted feelings to manage along with our decision (and that's when the process of Let it Be can help).

Finding Your Krewe

My father was born and raised in New Orleans, Louisiana, and is the first generation to have ever lived outside of the city since our family emigrated from Europe by way of Martinique. I grew up eating gumbo, jambalaya, etoufée, and red beans and rice (only with Camellia's red beans and pickle meat, of course). My earliest memories are of my parents' Mardi Gras parties, where every year I hoped I got the baby in the King Cake. And in the family photo album, there's a picture of me as an infant sipping from a can of Dixie beer. (I've been assured it was empty.)

A key part of New Orleans culture, particularly as it relates to Carnival season and Mardi Gras, is the krewe, an organization that sponsors and produces a parade, replete with floats, costumes, masks, and the ubiquitous beads. Some krewes are open to all who are willing to pay to help produce the parade, but for several of the oldest and most established krewes, you also have to be selected and successfully complete an initiation process. Each krewe has its own identity, which is often represented in the parade it sponsors. Many of the krewes are named after Greek and Roman gods. For example, the Krewe of Bacchus, one of the oldest and most historical krewes, celebrates Bacchus, the god of wine and drunkenness (this is New Orleans, after all!).

So what does a New Orleans krewe have to do with building your small business? Because as an entrepreneur, you have to create, nurture, and develop your own krewe. This is why we invest so much time, energy, and money into marketing: It's how we attract potential clients, build a relationship with them, and ultimately welcome them into our community—our krewe—by becoming a customer. And Determine What Matters can help.

Remember in Chapter 2 when we talked about the know like trust (KLT) factor? That's the process your potential client or customer goes through before they commit to buying your product or service. First, they need to get to *know* you—and not just you, but what you provide and the value it brings them. Then, they need to *like* you.

They have to feel good about you and what you're selling. Finally, they need to *trust* you, and believe that what you're offering will help them achieve the outcome they want. Without the KLT factor, you're unlikely to make the sale.

So how do you cultivate KLT and attract clients and customers? By starting with Determine What Matters. Once you know your business (and personal) values, you can infuse them into every decision and action you make in your business, including your marketing. By communicating your personal beliefs and values to your audience, you're inviting them to get to know you—and your business—better. By doing so, you're attracting people who identify with and share your values. You'll build alliances and credibility (aka like and trust) more quickly, and you'll do so in an authentic way.

It may seem counterintuitive, but attracting clients starts out as an inside job. First, you Determine What Matters to you and your business, which requires awareness and self-reflection. Then, the internal becomes external as you allow those values to inform the work you create and the message you deliver. That's how you build KLT, and that's how you find clients and build your krewe.

The Determine What Matters process isn't just for small businesses and entrepreneurs, either. It's used by companies and corporations of all sizes and all genres. I can't think of a better example of how to build—and destroy—KLT than Facebook.

With more than two billion users, one could argue that Facebook doesn't need to worry about finding its people; it already has an extraordinary group of users, right? But in an age when new social media platforms are emerging on the regular and familiar faces like Twitter and Snapchat are poised for continued growth, Facebook knows it needs to stay relevant and connected with its users to succeed.

Perhaps that's why in June 2017, the company unveiled its new mission statement: "To give people the power to build community and bring the world closer together."[4] In 14 words, Facebook not only shared the values that guide the company, but it did so in a way that built the KLT factor. Facebook infused the message with its core values of shared opportunity, community, connection, and growth, with the vision of empowering users and providing opportunities for connection. Ideally, this would lead to the development of a stronger sense of community and belonging, leading to growth of all kinds—from the individual user's personal and professional growth, to business user growth and, of course, Facebook's growth as well.

However, in order to maintain the KLT factor with your community, you have to continuously live out those values—and, as we've discovered, Facebook has failed to do so. Its algorithms have allowed false media reports and hoaxes (aka "fake news") to spread on its platform like wildfire, and some critics argue that the perpetuation of these stories on Facebook affected the results of the 2016 US presidential election.

And if that weren't bad enough, then came the Cambridge Analytica scandal. In March 2018, it was discovered that more than 87 million Facebook users had their data sold to Cambridge Analytica, a political data analysis firm. The way the data were collected was problematic, in that an app collected not only the data of the 270,000 people who volunteered to use the app, but also the data of their Facebook friends, who had not provided direct consent. In response, Mark Zuckerberg, founder and CEO of Facebook, issued a public apology for a breach of trust, and Facebook released an advertising campaign aimed at restoring public faith.

Although Facebook remains the predominant social media platform worldwide, its persona has taken a huge beating due in large part to that breach of trust. When trust in a company disappears, the KLT factor drops and it's hard to rebuild. Thousands of people abandoned Facebook and deleted their profiles. In other words, they left the krewe. It's yet to be determined whether Facebook can come back from this—it's become such an omnipresent part of our culture that it may be "too big to fail"—but it's safe to say its reputation is seriously tarnished.

Even though most of us aren't running billion-dollar businesses like Facebook, there's a lesson in this for all of us. You can create a strong vision and mission for your company when it's rooted in your business principles and personal values, and that will help you create your krewe and connect with the people you want to serve. But you cannot simply pay lip service to this concept; you have to live these values out every day (more about how to do this in Chapter 8). If you don't, you risk damaging your business by losing the trust of your clients and betraying your krewe.

Facing Your Fears

Determining What Matters also helps us face down our fears and the negative self-talk that keeps us stuck, because we're driven to keep going in the service of what matters most. Being an entrepreneur is an ironic struggle. On some level, we know that we have what it takes to create a successful business, yet most of us are plagued with self-doubt and uncertainty. We struggle with imposter syndrome, we feel like a fraud, we question whether we have the talent, or intelligence, or ability, or money to keep the whole operation running. It's enough to give anyone whiplash.

I've witnessed clients and friends succumb to those horrible inner voices. It's devastating to see someone with vision and talent become paralyzed by fear and doubt. In Chapter 9, we go into more detail about how to combat the barrage of negative self-talk and limiting beliefs, but I want to introduce the concept now because Determine What Matters is a key component of overcoming that paralysis. Because when we are clear on what matters most and how we want to live our lives, then we are better equipped to challenge our limiting beliefs and make progress toward our vision.

This book is an example of that.

I wanted to write this book because I know in my gut that the six core concepts of ACT are relevant not just in a psychological setting, but in business and in life. I've witnessed their power in my own life and the lives of my clients, and I believe that if entrepreneurs embrace these concepts, we can change the landscape of business. So I set a goal to write a book about this, and that goal is in alignment with my values of service, integrity, and love.

I had written 20,000 words of my first draft, finishing up the first section, and then I froze. I hit writer's block in a major way, and I couldn't bring myself to sit down and write. It was ridiculous, really. I had just written almost half of the book, and yet I was terrified to keep going. All of my inner trolls came out to play, telling me that I was a fraud, that my ideas were unoriginal, that my writing was derivative. I began to think that maybe I had set too great a goal—that writing a book wasn't really for me.

For four weeks, I didn't write a word. And for four weeks, I felt disconnected and unhappy. I knew writing this book was important and that I was letting my inner trolls keep me from moving forward. Yet still, I felt paralyzed and stuck.

And then, a miracle happened: the miracle of *Teen Titans Go!*

For those of you who are not the mother of 11- and 9-year-old boys, allow me to introduce you to *Teen Titans Go!* It's an animated show on The Cartoon Network, and it's quirky and smart and funny and wonderful. It's one of those rare kid shows that adults might actually enjoy, even if it is a little goofy and frenetic.

The morning of the miracle, my kids were watching *Teen Titans Go!* while I was getting ready. I was paying zero attention; it was merely background noise to my own incessant inner soundtrack of self-doubt and failure. (I told you, it was a rough four weeks.) But then, the voice of young Robin encouraging Cyborg cut through my mind's monologue:

"Just because you're scared doesn't mean you're not strong."[5]

Everything came to a full stop. I repeated it to myself out loud: Just because you're scared doesn't mean you're not strong. And with that, I remembered that even though I was scared of putting my thoughts on paper, of sharing my story, of being brave, I could be strong and do it anyway. That there are things worth doing even when we're scared, especially if they matter deeply to us. That when I'm living my core values, I can do anything.

So I got my ass back in my seat, in front of my laptop, and broke through my writer's block by writing this down.

This is why Determine What Matters is so important. It goes beyond setting goals and objectives; it creates a touchstone to guide you through the highs and lows of entrepreneurship and life. It's the first step in creating your vision and bringing it to life, and the foundation of every step after. There will be times when the storm rolls in and the fog descends, and your values seem distant or out of reach. But when you quiet the mind and connect with the spirit, your values become a beacon of light, cutting through the fog so that you can brave the storm. Even when that spirit comes via the voice of a cartoon character.

Going through Hell

Although Winston Churchill is best known as a politician, he was also one of the most prolific writers of his time. Whenever I read or hear a great unattributed quote, I always suspect it's a Churchill line (and it often is). His words are inspirational, clever, and often funny, as is my favorite line of his: "If you're going through hell, keep going." I've navigated my way through many difficult times with that quote, because it reminds me that no matter how bad things are, it won't last forever, and I can choose how to make my way through. That's especially important to Determine What Matters when dealing with difficulty, because when we're facing rough seas, our values are our anchor.

Shortly after I first learned about psychological flexibility and the six core processes, I was faced with a professional crisis that required me to put them to good use. I worked as a therapist for a company whose mission was important to me, and I loved the direct service components of my job. However, the work environment was obscenely toxic, and the structure and policies in my office often ran counter to the agency's mission. I literally would get nauseated on the way to work every day because I was so stressed and unhappy, and I dreamed of quitting.

So why did I stay as long as I did? Because the Determine What Matters process showed me that my value of service was top priority.

I believed in the mission of the agency, I wanted to help my clients, and I knew that, if I left, my clients would experience a lapse in care and I was concerned about their welfare. There were competing values at play, including care of the self, but up until I left, service to others won out. Every day, I reminded myself that I was there because I was a part of something bigger and that what I did made a positive impact in the lives of my clients. That really helped.

I held fast to that belief until I discovered that a colleague was making inappropriate comments to clients and exhibiting behavior that was negligent at best, egregious at worst. Based on what my clients shared with me, I was ethically obligated to file a complaint against my colleague alleging incompetent practice. The entire experience was miserable, and when the agency's version of disciplinary action was a paid suspension and written reprimand, I resigned in protest. That period of my life was one of the most difficult professional experiences I'd faced, but knowing I was true to my values and ethics helped me get through it. I served my clients as well as I could within the agency, and when I resigned, I did so in the hope that my departure would lead to structural change and improve client care. (The epilogue to the story? A year later, the colleague was fired for continued poor behavior and the supervisor regretted not being more assertive earlier.)

***

When we understand our purpose in life and are in touch with what's important, it's much easier to brave the storms. It doesn't get rid of the difficulties or magically improve the circumstances, but it does provide some relief. And from that space of relief, we free ourselves to move forward and take action that aligns with what matters to us.

TECHNIQUES TO DETERMINE WHAT MATTERS

At this point, we've covered what Determine What Matters is, why it's important, and the times when you might find it particularly useful. Now it's time to explore how to put the process into action— how to actually Determine What Matters. The good news is that there's no one prescription to follow, because there are an infinite number of ways you can identify what gives your life meaning and purpose. Just as each person has different values, there are different ways to uncover and clarify them.

In this section, I provide you with several exercises, and I encourage you to choose one or more of them to explore. How you choose to explore them is up to you. You may find journaling to be a valuable process, or you might prefer to use one of the exercises as a conversation prompt and engage in a discussion with a friend, colleague, coach, or mentor. Maybe one of the exercises will spark your creativity and you'll find a way to incorporate the expressive arts (painting, dance, drawing, whatever). Bottom line: There's no right or wrong way to approach an exercise. What matters is the intention you bring to the experience. My intention is that you find the following options helpful to Determine What Matters most to you.

What Makes You Happy

Close your eyes and think about a favorite moment—a time when you felt truly, completely content. Maybe it's one of those rare times when you were so fully present and immersed in the moment that time seemed to stand still. Take some time to remember the little details of that moment. Where were you? Who else was there? What were you doing? What stands out?

Some of my happiest memories involve my family: a day date with my husband, building a blanket fort and snuggling with my oldest son, taking my youngest son to an out-of-town soccer tournament and getting to spend one-on-one time with him. So it probably won't surprise you that love, connection, and family rank high on my list of values.

When you experience sheer happiness, I can almost guarantee that it's because you were living in harmony with your values. When your actions align with what matters most to you, then you create the ideal environment for happiness. If we frame that statement like an equation (values + actions = happiness), then we can reverse the equation and solve for values.

What Angers You

Think about a time when you got angry—like full-out, balls-to-the-wall angry. Remember the circumstances that prompted your response. Who was involved? What happened? How did you feel during and after the event?

When you get angry, it's often because one of your values was threatened. For example, if you got really, really angry when a car cut you off on the highway, that might indicate you value fairness and order. Or maybe you got blazing mad when your child told you that another kid made fun of them; that could indicate that you value family, or love, or justice. Something that makes my husband extraordinarily angry is when he feels like I've undermined him or his disciplinary style in front of our children. I suspect this means he values not only respect, but also partnership. When it appears that I go against him, he feels abandoned and alone.

If thinking about what makes us happy can help us focus on what matters, then so too can the things that make us unhappy.

One Day Left

Imagine that you've been told that tomorrow night, when you fall asleep, you will peacefully and painlessly transition from this world to the next. The next 24 hours will be your last on this earth, and you can spend them however you choose. Where will you spend your last day? What will you do? With whom, if anyone, will you spend it? Take your time and fully envision your final day alive.

Once you know how you would spend your last day, down the final detail, step back and look at where you decided to be, what you decided to do, and with whom you decided to spend your day. What does that tell you about what matters most to you? For example, if you chose to spend the day at home with your partner and your children, perhaps you value family and love. If you decided to go skydiving or another bucket list activity, maybe you value adventure and growth. If you opted to contact the people who changed your life to let them know their impact, perhaps you value gratitude and connection.

This exercise asks you to view time as a limited resource. How you choose to use that limited resource will tell you a great deal about what matters most to you, and what gives your life meaning.

Your Biggest Regret

Close your eyes, take a deep breath, and remember a time when you did something you regretted and felt ashamed—or perhaps when you failed to do something, and you wish you had. Where were you? Was anyone else involved? What influenced your choice? What would you do differently today?

This is a tough exercise, because I'm asking you to tap into the feeling of shame. Shame is an extraordinarily powerful feeling that most people avoid, and I acknowledge your willingness to reexperience shame in the service of connecting with what matters most to you. If there's an upside to shame, it's that it can help us connect with a deep belief that we've violated. If we feel shame because we spread gossip about a coworker, then we know we've not lived out our value of honesty. If the shame monster rears its ugly head when we yell at our partner or child, then we're not practicing our value of love.

In her TED Talk,[6] Brené Brown differentiates between guilt and shame by proposing that guilt is focused on behavior, whereas shame is focused on the self. Brown says, "Shame is, 'I am bad.' Guilt is, 'I did something bad.'" Once you've tapped into that feeling of shame and identified the value beneath it, please offer yourself compassion and understanding. You are not defined solely by your actions, and you are not a bad person because you made a mistake. Acknowledge the mistake, ask for forgiveness if appropriate, and recommit to living in accordance with what matters most to you. (The rest of this book can help you do that.)

The People You Admire

Think of someone you really admire, someone whose presence, personality, and behavior you'd want to emulate. This could be someone you know personally, or maybe it's a celebrity, a politician, or a thought leader. It could even be a fictional character from a book, movie, television show, or play. As long as this person represents an ideal and embodies qualities you'd want for yourself, you can choose anyone you want.

Once you have a clear image of this person in your mind, ask yourself: What do I like most about them? What do they talk about or do that connects with me? What attributes do they possess that I'd like to grow in myself? Reflect on your answers and search for the values implicit in your response. What do you think matters most to them? To what extent do those values resonate with you?

Sometimes, when you feel uncertain or unclear about your personal values, it helps to take an outside perspective. Identifying what matters most to someone you respect or with whom you feel a connection can help uncover what matters most to you.

Your Eulogy

Imagine that you've reached the end of your life. You've lived a long, full, rewarding life, and you've accomplished everything you ever wanted. At your funeral are all the people you love and who loved you, and everyone whose lives you've touched and improved. Although everyone is sad that you're gone, the mood is also light, as people are expressing their gratitude for your presence in their lives and celebrating all that you were.

Now, your most beloved person begins to deliver your eulogy. This person is describing you and how you lived your life. Who is this person? What are they saying? What stories do they share about you? What words, feelings, and images do they use to describe you? What are the values implicit in the memories they share?

By creating a future projection of yourself in which you've lived a life of your dreams, you can identify the values you want to bring forth today. And by viewing yourself through the eyes of someone who deeply loves you, you might uncover new values in yourself.

CHAPTER 8

Make it So

WHAT IS MAKE IT SO?

In this chapter, I walk you through what is both the easiest and most difficult of the six processes: Make it So. It's easy in the sense that the process is not complicated. Once you know your values, it's simply a matter of aligning your actions with them. And yet, so many people find it difficult to take the first step. Whether it's external obstacles, inner blocks, or a combination of the two, there are plenty of reasons (and excuses) why we don't take action in our lives—which is why I devote the next two chapters to exploring how to respond to inner blocks. However, this chapter focuses on specific strategies to help you take action that's consistent with your values.

Consistency is at the core of Make it So, both in terms of values and action. This process is all about developing systems and routines to help you act in a manner that's congruent with what matters most to you. When your choices are in alignment with your priorities, you demonstrate consistency between what you believe and how you act. And when what you say and do reflect who you are and what you believe, you're far more likely to find business success and personal fulfillment. Simply put, the more consistency between your actions and your values, the happier you'll be.

This is why being clear on your why is a critical first step in developing any sort of action plan. If you're not sure of your *why*, then you're going to have problems with your *how*. You might get some traction and make some progress, but you're only going to get so far. You can have all the tools, resources, money, and time at your disposal, but if you don't know why you're doing something—or you don't believe you can do something—it ain't happenin'.

The rest of this chapter walks you through why Make it So is a core process for entrepreneurs and how to put it into practice. And if you've already completed the Determine What Matters process, you've got a head start on your business success. So let's examine why it's important for entrepreneurs to Make it So, and then I'll share with you the exact process I used to get back in sync with my business.

WHY IS MAKE IT SO IMPORTANT?

On the surface, it might seem obvious why Make it So is a critical process for entrepreneurs to practice. If we're not taking action, then we're probably not generating revenue, and if we're not generating revenue, then we won't be in business for very long. However, there are other, slightly more subtle reasons why Make it So is important in business. Even though it's an outward process that's focused more on *doing*, Make it So remains connected with our internal processor—the mind—and can influence our *being*.

Maintaining Mindset

I've noticed an interesting pattern when coaching entrepreneurs. Without exception, every one of my clients inherently knows that taking action is critical to success, and yet they still struggle to do it. (Often, it's because they are hampered by inner criticism and a lack of confidence; we get into those issues in the next few chapters.) Even after they've done some inner work and started to develop their business mindset, they're surprised at how difficult it can be to actually take the next step, and the step after that, and the step after that. Their expectation is that once they get the mindset piece down, they'll be good to go. If only that were the case.

The fact is, mindset work is not a "one and done" event. It's something you will continue to do for the rest of your life, because you're always changing and growing. Your mind will never stop doing what it does best: churning out all of those fears and doubts to "help" you prepare for the worst. And if the mind really does its job well, you'll decide to stay safe and not do anything. (Don't worry. That's where the core processes of Create Space and Let it Be can help. Those are coming up next.)

Remember: Your task is not to stop the mind from doing its job. It's simply to be aware of what it's doing (and why it's doing it), and to decide the extent to which it will dictate your behavior. If you don't want it to control your actions, then you need to have another strategy in place—and that's where Make it So comes in. Developing methods to Make it So will help you maintain your entrepreneurial mindset and stave off anxiety, uncertainty, and fear. The systems you create to build a business that matters will help combat any "stinkin' thinkin'" that your mind generates. In fact, as you practice and perfect your systems, they become second nature and crowd out the limiting beliefs and negative self-talk your mind feeds you.

Getting Unstuck

Even still, it takes more than a positive mindset to Make it So. It also requires having systems in place that support you and your business, so that taking value-based action becomes routine. By having clear processes for goal-setting and decision-making that are in sync with what matters to you, you'll be able to bring your vision to life in an efficient yet heart-centered manner. Without a clear strategy, you run the risk of falling into the Sisyphus Effect—taking action that's inconsistent with who you are and what matters to you, which can undermine your vision and keep you from making progress.

In my work with entrepreneurs, I've noticed a few patterns when it comes to getting stuck. See if you identify with any of these experiences:

- You have an idea and you are off to the races! You've hit the ground running and you're ready to go. You've got a vision, you've got a mission, and you are going to *make shit happen.* And you do—for a week, or maybe two. Then things start to taper off and you lose steam. That amazing newsletter you started hasn't gone out in weeks. Those daily Instagram posts fall off to one or two a week. Your weekly Facebook Live has become a monthly feature, if that. As your momentum tanks, so too does your faith in yourself and your ability to build your business. A few months go by until inspiration strikes, and you recommit yourself to your work and the frenetic cycle starts again.

- You have an idea for your business and you're excited to put it into place. But you don't want to implement it incorrectly, because getting it right from the beginning will save time, energy, and money. So you focus on research, planning, and prep, making sure all of your Is are dotted and Ts are crossed. You're on your seventeenth draft of your web copy, and you don't want to publish your sales page until it's perfect. Meanwhile, your expenses are piling up and there's no revenue coming in. You feel stuck and fearful, and you're thinking about abandoning the idea altogether. Eventually, you move forward, dissatisfied that the end result isn't as good as you want it to be.

- Things in your business are . . . fine. Really. You're doing okay. You've got some clients, you've got some routines, and for the most part you know where you're heading. You're doing all the things you're supposed to do: You're blogging/vlogging/ podcasting regularly, you're active on social media, you're networking. You've got it down pat. So why does it all feel so mundane? You went into business for yourself because you wanted the energy and excitement of being your own boss. And even though you're not punching in and out on a time clock, everything feels like an obligation.

At some point, many of us have experienced one (or more) of these scenarios, each one being some manifestation of the Sisyphus Effect. Whether you tend to struggle with consistency, perfectionism, or boredom, Make it So can help. If you're someone who tends to start strong only to flame out, then it's particularly important to develop sustainable systems that promote consistency. If you have difficulty moving forward if things aren't 100% perfect, then adopting a method that rewards action and encourages assessment will be key. And if you're susceptible to boredom, then you'll want to make sure you keep your purpose—your big why—front and center at all times. As a process, Make it So is both comprehensive and flexible, so that it can address all of these potential pitfalls and then some.

Finding Balance

In addition to dealing with perfectionism, consistency, boredom, inner critics, and negative thinking, entrepreneurs also have to manage another important factor: time. Entrepreneurs are some of the busiest people I've ever known. We're juggling multiple roles in our businesses, trying to do all the things; and on top of that, we have lives outside of our businesses. We are partners, parents, children, friends, and volunteers. We have responsibilities and obligations to other people that we have to balance with our work life, and somewhere in all of that, we also need to carve out time just for ourselves. Whether it's a doctor's appointment, a yoga class, or a glass of wine and a book at the end of the day, we've got to take care of ourselves physically, mentally, and spiritually—and the frenetic pace of entrepreneurship can make that exceptionally difficult. How do we balance it all?

Ah, there's that buzzword: *balance*. It comes up in almost every discussion I have with my clients and colleagues, and everyone seems to be trying (and failing) to achieve that elusive prize of work-life balance. We've been conditioned to think that work-life balance is something we can achieve, if only we have the right program/system/iPhone/powdered shake mix. If we just keep trying, one day we'll achieve balance and everything will be bliss.

Truth time: There is no such thing as achieving balance, because balance isn't a constant. It's a process, a series of micro-adjustments that we're constantly making in order to achieve stasis. Imagine you're on a balance beam and you want to walk from one end to the other. In order to do so, your body engages in myriad small movements to keep you from falling off the beam. Some movements you're aware of, and some are automatic. But if your body stops doing them, you'll freeze and fall off the beam. You'll lose your balance.

The same is true in life. Every day is a series of adjustments to make it across the beam. Some days, we feel like we have it down pat and everything works so that we make it across. Other days, it's a train wreck, we feel overwhelmed and lost, and we fall off. But if we stop midway, we get stuck and we're likely to fall off. Even though there are no guarantees, we have to keep moving in order to make it across.

If there's one thing I want you take away from this chapter, it's this: It is not possible to achieve permanent work-life balance, because balance isn't a "one and done" activity. It's a series of actions we mindfully take that help us stay true to what matters most. And this is where it gets tricky, because even though many of us know on an intellectual level that finding permanent balance isn't possible, we continue to search and strive for it. We (unconsciously) buy into the illusion that we're just one yoga class, one big client, one diet cleanse away. So when those things fail to bring us into a state of perpetual and perfect bliss, we internalize that failure and believe we are the problem. And then we look for something or someone else to help us feel more balanced and aligned, and the vicious cycle continues.

This is why Make it So is a particularly important core process for entrepreneurs, because it breaks the cycle. It's not about achieving an unrealistic expectation of balance. It's about choosing a different approach and creating a system anchored in your values so that you're taking wise steps in your business. This ensures your actions are efficient *and* consistent with what's important to you. Your system will keep you from spinning your wheels and wasting time, which prevents unnecessary stress, frustration, and despair. It also ensures that the work you're doing matters to you, so at the end of the day, you feel good about what you've accomplished.

TECHNIQUES TO MAKE IT SO

Now that we understand the what and the why behind Make it So, it's time to talk about how to implement it. When it comes to creating growth and success in your business, this process is paramount. After all, if you don't convert all of this great insight you've developed about yourself and your vision into action, then what's the point? Sure, it's wonderful to know yourself better and gain clarity about what's important to you, but if that doesn't translate into action, then you're not going to make any progress in your business.

In Acceptance and Commitment Therapy, the formal term for this process is called Committed Action, because it's all about committing to yourself and your values and translating that commitment into doing. It's helpful to start with Determine What Matters, because that allows us to calibrate our inner compass before we begin the journey toward what we want most in our businesses and our lives. Once we're clear on how we want to be, then we can get down to what we want to do.

I've developed a four-step system to guide you through the Make it So process, and it all starts with an **IDEA**:

Identify the goal.
Develop a plan.
Engage with purpose.
Assess the process and results.

Each aspect of IDEA builds on the previous step to help you bring your vision to life and Make it So. IDEA is intended to be implemented in a specific order: identify, then develop, then engage, then assess. However, if you find you're getting tripped up on a step, it's okay to go backward and fine-tune your process. There's no one way to implement IDEA, and I provide suggestions within each step to help you turn this system into your own. What's most important is making sure the actions you take are grounded in your values, consistent with your vision, and achievable in your business.

I could walk you through the process theoretically and talk about what you could do or should do to make this work in your business. But with a system like this, it helps to have a real-world example. I'm going to use myself and how I used the IDEA system to create this book as an example. Think of it as a behind-the-scenes tour of *ACT on Your Business*. You'll learn firsthand how I used IDEA to bring this book to life, and how IDEA helped me get back on track when my train derailed. You'll understand how to apply the steps to your own business and combat the Sisyphus Effect, and by following along in my journey, perhaps you'll avoid the pitfalls I encountered along the way.

So . . . are you ready to start a new IDEA?

Identify the Goal

The first step in the IDEA system is to identify the goal: What is it that you want to achieve? Now, maybe you've heard that your goals should be reasonable and achievable (more on that in a bit), and that's good advice, *but* having reasonable, achievable goals is the *result* of this step, not the starting point. Think of it as reverse-engineering your goal: start broad with your vision, and then narrow down to a smaller, achievable goal.

When I started with my IDEA, my business vision was to expand my coaching practice in order to help more entrepreneurs and small business owners live happy, successful lives. Super broad, right? So I had to narrow it down. A good old-fashioned brainstorm revealed a ton of ways I could help lots of people at once: I could create a group coaching program, I could develop a course, I could book speaking gigs, and so forth. All of these are great goals, and ones I might pursue in the future. But I knew I really wanted to write a book, because not only is writing a book a major bucket list item for me, but a book will allow me to share my message quickly and help as many people as possible. So there you have it: I developed the goal of writing a book in order to manifest my vision of expanding my coaching practice.

Once most people have a main goal, they move straight to the next step of creating a plan. We'll get there, but there's one important thing to do before we move forward, and that's checking in with what matters. It's critical to double-check that your goal is consistent with your values, and identify any potential value clashes that could emerge. If the goal works seamlessly with your values, then you move on to the next step. If not, then you pause and refine the goal.

When I decided I wanted to write a book, I asked myself a few questions: Is this goal consistent with who I am and what matters most to me? Will it allow me to show up authentically and grow my business at the same time? Is writing a book an expression of my values? To answer those questions, I went back to a pledge I made when I set my intentions for the year: to prioritize the values of service, connection, and love. Writing a book would help me *serve* entrepreneurs and small business owners by helping them achieve the success they want. It would build *connection* between my readers and me, and hopefully between other entrepreneurs and me as well. And it would foster *love*, because I view this book as a love letter to my ideal client. Not only will it help her create a business and a life she loves, but it's also an expression of what I love to do. Writing a book serves all three of my core values, so this is a goal worthy of my pursuit.

As you reflect on your vision and brainstorm goals for your business, you might not be sure which goal is appropriate to pursue. Perhaps you have so many possibilities, it's hard to narrow it down to just one. Or maybe you're feeling stuck and not sure where to begin. If that's the case, then I recommend using the Wheel of Life, a tool that will help you assess your satisfaction in different areas of your business and your life. (I've included a copy as this book's Appendix.[7])

To use the Wheel of Life, simply circle the number that reflects how satisfied you are in that domain, with 1 being "not satisfied at all" and 10 being "completely satisfied." After you've circled a number for all the domains, connect them to create your own wheel. This is a visual snapshot of your overall balance in your life. Then ask yourself: If this were a wheel on a bicycle, how smooth would my ride be? What areas would benefit from action, in order to create a more even ride? After you've selected a domain to focus on, you can identify your goal accordingly.

If you're still feeling stuck, then this is a great time to call out your reinforcements. Find a friend, family member, or colleague to whom you can talk about your next steps. Reach out to a business coach who can walk you through the process of clarifying your vision and brainstorming possible goals. You don't have to do this alone, and getting feedback and support from someone you trust can help ensure a strong start.

Once you know what you want to achieve, and can articulate why it matters to you and how it serves your vision, then you're ready for the next step. Get ready, honey: It's time to make a plan.

Develop a Plan

You've identified a goal—excellent! Now it's time to develop a plan to get it done. Building a comprehensive plan at the start will help you stay on track and in alignment with your why, all while creating a sense of accomplishment from hitting your benchmarks. It also provides peace of mind, knowing that you've not only got the skills, talents, and abilities to achieve your goal, but you've also got a system to make it happen. Trust me: That goes a looong way toward quieting the inner critic.

Having a plan also promotes sustainable action, which is critical for those of us who tend to go all-in at the start and then flame out. And when I say us, I mean it; this is definitely a tendency of mine. I have an unfortunate history of starting projects with vigor and then losing steam. When I was in my 20s, it was jewelry-making. In my early 30s, it was running. Most recently, it was knitting. (Please don't ask me about the huge box of yarn in my attic.)

But here's the great thing: Even if that's your history, it doesn't have to be your future. You are not defined by what you've done or failed to do in the past. Today is a new day, and you have the power to chart your own course forward, no matter how rocky the terrain behind you may have been. This was the case for me with running. After several years my running shoes gathering dust in my closet, the tragedy of the Boston Marathon bombing in April 2013 got me back out on the road. Knowing that I had two good legs and the ability to run when others had just had that ability robbed from them—well, my excuses were gone. I was out running (well, run-walking) that day.

However, I knew my tendency was to start strong and flame out, and I didn't want to do that again, particularly in light of what got me running again. Yet I needed more than that initial spark of inspiration to maintain my consistency, so I got on a training plan and stuck to it with the help of a few running buddies/accountability partners. And guess what? Six months later, I finished my first half-marathon. I was—and remain—slow as molasses, but I finished despite having several false starts (pun intended) in years past, and the key for me was having a plan and having support. This realization holds true in my business as well. With a solid plan and accountability in the form of a coach and a mastermind group, I choose to finish what I start.

When it comes to developing a plan, I recommend continuing to reverse-engineer what you want. With your goal as the end point, work backward and identify the sub-goals within it, then the objectives within those. Continue to break it down, until you've got a workable strategy built on small action steps. From there you can create a time line, starting with the date by which you want to achieve your larger goal, and then work backward toward today.

Let's go back to my example of writing this book. I'll be honest: Once I decided I wanted to write it, overwhelm set in and the inner critic came out to play. I get deeper into how to manage that in the next chapters, but for now, know that developing an action plan was vital in vanquishing my doubts and believing in myself. When I had a plan in front of me—a workable plan with specific steps and dates—all of a sudden, it became possible. And not just possible, but doable. I could write a book. The proof was right there in front of me! So if the mere thought of developing a plan brings out your own gremlins, just know that's a normal part of the process, and I've got you covered. But first, let's talk planning.

I started by defining what "writing a book" would entail. Of course, it meant actually writing something, but it also meant getting a book into the hands of the people I want to read it, which requires publishing and marketing it. So there were my three sub-goals: writing, publishing, and marketing. I chose to focus on the first sub-goal of actually writing the book for obvious reasons: If I didn't have a product to publish and market, then the plan would fall apart.

Then I went one level deeper and asked myself: What will it take to achieve the sub-goal of writing a book? Being a first-time author, I wasn't 100% sure, so I sought some guidance from a phenomenal developmental editor who would become my book coach. With her help, I realized that writing my book would mean finishing a rough draft, editing the first draft into a second draft, requesting beta reader feedback, incorporating feedback into a third draft, and then finalizing it for publication.

I continued to narrow the focus of my plan, starting with the first component: the rough draft. What goes into writing a first draft? Well, I'd need to come up with a topic, complete some preliminary research, create an outline, and start writing. That was about as specific as I wanted to be, so from there I created a time line based on when I wanted the book to be done. I set anticipated completion dates for each of those elements, and for the higher order elements as well.

This all sounds nice and neat and organized, doesn't it? Well, here's the truth: It wasn't always so organized. As I mentioned before, I had a major case of writer's block about halfway through writing the first draft, and I needed to take a little time off from writing. When I was ready to start writing again, I had to revisit my plan, change some dates, and recommit myself to the process. Having a plan won't protect you from the external and internal roadblocks that may throw you off course, but it will make it easier for you to course-correct.

Once you've developed a plan and gotten specific about how you'll achieve your goal, there's one more thing to consider before you press play, and that's workability. To what extent are these tasks and deadlines workable? Is this a reasonable plan, or are you biting off more than you can chew? To determine the answer, this is where the concept of SMART goals can help. You may already be familiar with SMART goals. This acronym has been around since the early 1980s, and although there are some minor variations, it generally stands for:

- **Specific.** How clear is the goal? For example, "I will be more successful in my business" is vague. "I will add a new revenue stream to my business and increase profitability by 15%" is much more specific.
- **Measurable.** How will you know when the goal is achieved? (Tip: The more specific the goal, the easier it is to measure.)
- **Achievable.** Is this something that can be accomplished? Is it within your power to do this? What are the steps to achieve it?
- **Realistic.** How likely is it that you can accomplish the goal? Do you have the resources you need to get it done?
- **Time-Limited.** Do you have a deadline by when you will accomplish this goal?

It's helpful to run your goal through the SMART factors to make sure it's workable. However, in *ACT Made Simple*, Russ Harris proposes an alternate definition of SMART goals that is more aligned with values-based goal-setting and decision-making. The S, R, and T remain the same, but he advises that goals should be meaningful (M) and adaptive (A). If your goal is meaningful, then it's guided by your values and adds a greater sense of meaning to your life. For a goal to be adaptive, it should move you in a direction that will improve or enhance your life.

The method I just described—reverse-engineering your goals, setting deadlines, and verifying they're SMART goals—is one way to develop a solid action plan. But it's certainly not the only way, and it may not be the best way for you. I encourage you to approach planning with a sense of curiosity, flexibility, and openness to see what will work best for you. And however you go about creating a plan, remember that even the most-detailed plans are subject to the slings and arrows of life. If something happens that forces you to go off-plan, it doesn't mean you're a failure or that you won't accomplish your goal. It simply means that your plan didn't cover that factor, but now you can account for it. That's all part of the process.

Engage with Purpose

Okay, my friend. You've identified your goal, you've developed your plan, and now you're finally ready to take action and do this thing. It's time to engage with purpose and achieve your goal. Blinders off, gates open, go to it! You got this!

All right, so maybe there's a little more to it than that. Engaging with purpose goes beyond "just do it." It means fully investing in what you're doing, bringing your complete attention and intention to your work. You are completely, totally present in the moment, and you know exactly what you're doing and why you're doing it. You're not taking action just for action's sake (or just because the plan says to do it). You're doing something because you are deeply connected to your why, and taking action is your way of manifesting your purpose and values. This is your soul's work, baby. This is love.

Spoiler alert: This is another one of those simple-but-not-easy tasks. It's not easy to consistently engage with purpose. Sometimes things feel boring or difficult or frustrating, and the last thing we want to do is show up and do the work. I totally get it. It happens to me, too, including while writing this book. I'm passionate about helping entrepreneurs introduce meaning, mindset, and mindfulness into their work. I believe it's the most powerful way to run your business and life your life, and I want everyone to know it. And yet sometimes, the thought of sitting down and typing words onto a screen made me want to throw my laptop out the window.

So what should you do when this happens? The answer is going to be different for everyone, but I'll share some of the things I do. Sometimes I meditate before getting down to work, so that I'm approaching my writing with a clear head. Sometimes I choose to work on a blog post or other project first, something that's still in line with what matters to me and that will push the needle forward in my business. Sometimes I take a break and go for a walk, or play with my kids, or binge watch *The Office* on Netflix. (I watched every single episode while writing this book. Jim and Pam 4eva.)

Whatever you do, please try to offer yourself some grace and space. You're human, and just because you know what to do (and why you're doing it), it doesn't mean you'll be able to every day. Some days you'll feel like your soul is on fire and everything you do happens quickly and with ease. And some days it will feel like a miracle to create a single sentence. That's all part of the process. It's all okay. Just keep showing up, and keep offering yourself compassion. Little by little, the work will get done.

There's not a lot more for me to say on this, because you've already done most of the heavy lifting. You're clear on your why, you know what you want, and you've figured out how to get it. Now it's simply time to put your head down, follow the plan, and do the work. You've got everything you need to make your goals a reality, and you know where to go for support if you need it. So get to it.

Assess the Process and Results

You did it! **Pops bottle of champagne** Congratulations! You chose a goal, you created a plan, and you put that plan into action. I knew you could do it; you had it in you all along. Maybe you accomplished your goal, or maybe you're well on your way to achieving it, or maybe it didn't work out quite how you planned. That's okay. Whatever happened, it doesn't end here. There's one more step for you to finish before you start your next big IDEA. It's time for a little reflection and assessment.

This step is particularly reassuring for those of us who struggle with perfectionism and who fear putting anything out into the world before it's done. When you build an assessment strategy into your process, it removes some of the pressure to be perfect. You can move forward, confident in the knowledge that you've got a system in place to address any perceived problems, either during or after the project. Consider the assessment your safety net, allowing you to take big, bold action, but there in case you need it.

There's no single correct way to assess your process and results, so feel free to try different options and make it your own. One assessment option is a SWOT analysis: strengths (S), weaknesses (W), opportunities (O), and threats (T). SWOT has been around since the 1960s and 1970s, and though it's typically used as a strategic planning tool, it also works well during and after a project. It provides a solid framework to objectively assess your efforts and uncover what worked, what didn't, what you could do next, and what you need to watch out for. It's often helpful to think of strengths and weaknesses as things that are internal to you or your business, and opportunities and threats as things that are external. Here are a few questions that might be a part of your SWOT process:

Strengths
- What did you do particularly well?
- What sets you apart from other people or companies doing what you do?
- What resources did you use particularly well?
- What positive results did you see?

Weaknesses
- What didn't work out?
- What could you improve upon?
- What would you differently next time?

Opportunities
- What new opportunities did this goal or project generate?
- How could achieving this goal lead to other possibilities?

Threats
- What obstacles came up as you were working toward this goal?
- How might changes in your niche, your industry, technology affect your business?
- What are other people or companies in your industry doing?
- To what extent could the weaknesses you identified adversely affect your business?

As helpful as a SWOT analysis can be, there's one thing I believe it lacks, and that is heart. Its strength is its objectivity, but that means it doesn't fully address the emotional and spiritual aspects of working toward a goal. I would propose adding another category addressing the relational component of your project, although then you'd have SWOTR. Or worse, WORTS, which would be the worst acronym ever. Yet I would also consider the following questions:

Relational
- How did working toward this goal make you feel?
- To what extent did working on this goal allow you to live out your values?
- Was there anyone who was particularly helpful (or unhelpful) in this process?

The truth is, you don't have to wait until the end of your plan to take action on this last step. Ideally, you'll be assessing your plan as you go, so you can fine-tune it and make any changes you need in the moment. But sometimes, we need a little time and space from a project before we're able to accurately assess how things went, so if this step does come at the end of your plan, that's okay too. But please don't skip this step, even if everything worked out perfectly. There's so much to learn from a project, regardless of whether it's a total success, a complete failure, or something in between. There are opportunities and lessons in everything we do, and assessing both your results *and* your process can help you now and as your business grows.

***

Make it So is a flexible, adaptable process that you can use for anything and everything. Regardless of what you choose to do in your business and your life, applying the IDEA system will help you accomplish any goal you want. Make it So builds upon Determine What Matters so that whatever you choose to do, you can do so from a place of meaning and purpose. There's no limit to what you can accomplish, my friend. So go out there and do it.

CHAPTER 9

Create Space

WHAT IS CREATE SPACE?

Although all six core processes are integral to building your entrepreneurial flexibility, I believe that Create Space is the most revolutionary. It will completely change the way you relate to your thoughts, your mind, and yourself, which in turn will affect how you interact with other people and how you view the world around you. Although each process works with the others to build your entrepreneurial flexibility, Create Space is the linchpin holding it all together. It is the foundational process for increasing your mental resilience, and with greater resilience comes an increased sense of competence and confidence, as well as an improved ability to regain your footing after a misstep or unexpected event.

When you Create Space, you increase the separation between your thoughts and your self-concept, or your identity. Now, bear with me, because I recognize what I'm about to say might be a little radical or new age-y, but I'm going to say it anyway: *You are not your thoughts.*

Let me explain. Your mind is an incredibly powerful meaning-making machine. Your mind is constantly churning out new thoughts, new ideas, and, yes, new judgments. Sometimes it's about things that have already happened; maybe you're getting caught up in the past or ruminating over choices you've made. Sometimes it's about what's yet to come; maybe you're predicting the future or worrying about something that hasn't happened yet.

This is part of the mind's desire to keep you safe. If you've done something wrong in the past, it wants to make sure you're not going to do it again, so you go into instant replay mode and play the tape over . . . and over . . . and over until you learn not to do it again. Likewise, if there's something coming up in the future that could threaten the status quo, your mind is going to lead you through it in advance to make sure you do it right. You'll create all sorts of possible options or outcomes—even terrible, horrible, awful ones—because the mind is in safety monitor mode. You'll be prepared for the worst.

When this happens, it's very easy for these thoughts to become part of your reality and part of your identity. You can identify with them so strongly that not only do you believe them, you become them. Your identity fuses with your thoughts, so that you view everything your mind creates as truth.

But here's the thing: You are not your thoughts. Or, to quote Eckhardt Tolle, "You are not your mind." Your mind is a part of you, as are your thoughts, but they are not all of you, any more than your leg or your hair or your teeth are all of you. The minute we realize our minds don't have to define us, then we regain a sense of agency or control over how we view ourselves and the behaviors we choose to have.

This is where the third M—mindfulness—comes in. Mindfulness practice helps create separation between the thought and the self. It enables us to realize that we may have thoughts and we may have feelings, but we are not our thoughts and we are not our feelings. When you do that, you Create Space between what you think and who you are, and in that space exists the possibility of choice. By noticing your thoughts without attaching to them, you can decide the extent to which your thoughts influence your actions. You can move forward from a place where you choose our actions instead of resorting to default mode. You empower yourself to Determine What Matters and Make it So, regardless of what thoughts your mind might be feeding you.

As we explore the *what*, *why*, and *how* of Create Space, it's important to remember that you are not your mind. Or maybe a better way to say it is, you are not *just* your mind. Yes, your mind is an incredible creation, capable of generating all sorts of ideas, stories, judgments, rationales, and products. Your mind receives, processes, and interprets millions of data points to help you make decisions and take action. Sometimes you're aware of this; often you're not. And because the mind helps us make sense of the world, it's easy to think of the mind as the self. But it's not. It's just one component. An important component, but not the only one.

And yet, it's so easy to get lost in your thoughts and believe everything your mind tells you. When this happens, you're experiencing the shadow process of Create Space. You are Getting Hooked, or, in ACT language, Cognitive Fusion. Think about a welder using heat to fuse two pieces of metal. The heat creates a bond between them so that the two pieces become one. This is basically what happens when you Get Hooked: Your thoughts fuse with your identity so that they become seemingly inseparable. Your mind hooks you into believing what you think is who you are, and it turns up the heat by churning out thought after thought after thought.

So how do you turn down the heat and stop fusing your mind with yourself? You Create Space. You notice your thoughts without attaching to them, and by doing so, you start to peel the thought away from the judgment, like peeling old nail polish off your thumbnail. You create a place for those thoughts to exist without buying into them. You recognize that a thought by itself is simply a string of words and images; it has no inherent meaning or value. Its meaning comes from your perception and judgment. You let them come— and you let them go.

Sounds amazing, right? It is, and it works. But if you're giving me some skeptical side-eye right now, I get it. I'm asking you to completely change how you relate to your thoughts, and that probably feels radical and maybe even a little woo-woo. Later in this chapter, I walk you through several tools to help you Create Space, and you can choose the one(s) that work best for you. These techniques are easy to apply, have immediate benefit, and, with practice, will become second nature. It might feel weird to practice them at first, which makes sense. It feels strange and uncomfortable the first time you do anything new, whether you're riding a bike, cooking a new recipe, or starting a new business. The same is true with Create Space, so if this is new territory for you, a little discomfort is expected (and normal).

I'm inviting you to retrain how you communicate with your mind and how your mind communicates with you. In doing so, you are fundamentally changing your mind and strengthening your growth mindset. Remember in Chapter 2, when I discussed Carol Dweck's groundbreaking work in mindset? Having a growth mindset allows us to better adapt to change and move forward in our lives, and this is at the heart of entrepreneurial flexibility, particularly as it relates to openness to opportunity. Entrepreneurs with growth mindsets don't view the world through the lens of right and wrong. They have the ability to see everything that happens as an opportunity, even if it comes from a mistake. In fact, from a growth mindset perspective, there are no mistakes—just possibilities for growth and development.

When you practice the process of Create Space, you are separating the judgment from the thought, and the thought from the self. You will no longer view life through the narrow lens of good and bad, but instead through the wide lens of opportunity. You'll release yourself from automatically judging things as right or wrong, including yourself. You'll be able to view your own thoughts from a neutral place, knowing that thoughts are just words and images, and that the power of ascribing meaning to them is yours.

Let that last part sink in. You, and you alone, have the ability to give your thoughts meaning and to determine their relevance and importance in your life. No one else can do this for you—not your parents, not your partner, not your boss, not your teacher, not society. No one decides what your thoughts mean—and how much they mean—but you. It's the superpower of discernment, knowing what and how much meaning every thought holds. You may accept a thought, or reject it. You decide whether it's important, or not. It's all up to you. And that power is nothing short of revolutionary. It's what will change the world.

WHY IS CREATE SPACE IMPORTANT?

Before we get into the how of Create Space, let's get clear on why it's important and when practicing this process is most helpful. While we can Create Space any time we choose, it's particularly relevant during those times in which we get caught up in our thoughts and start to believe them. This is the shadow process, Getting Hooked. In *ACT Made Simple*, Russ Harris describes six main areas where we tend to fuse with our thoughts and fall into the Getting Hooked trap: rules, reasons, judgments, past, future, and self. Let's take a look at each of those six areas and how entrepreneurs may be particularly vulnerable to each.

Rules

Each one of us has a set of rules by which we live our lives. Some of these rules we set consciously, such as no caffeine after 5 p.m. or not buying another online course until we finish the ones we've already purchased (sigh). But there are also rules that guide the choices we make and actions we take, and we're not aware of them. And this lack of awareness can seriously hamper our ability to create change in our lives.

Here are a few rules my clients have uncovered for themselves. Notice if any of them resonate with you:

- If it's not perfect, it's not worth doing.
- I can't start a business until I know exactly what I'm doing.
- Being a business owner shouldn't be this hard.
- I shouldn't feel so nervous about doing something I love.
- My clients should do what I tell them to do.
- I'm an entrepreneur. I shouldn't feel like this.

These rules often have a lot to do with what we should or shouldn't do, or how we should or shouldn't feel. Anytime my client utters the word *should* in a session, we hit the brakes hard and explore the rule underneath it. This idea that you shouldn't feel this way—where did that come from? Who or what told you that? How has this rule held you back? What's another way to approach this situation? What new rule would you like to create for yourself?

Rules are not inherently bad; in fact, they can provide structure and guidance when you most need them. However, rules can be problematic when you fuse so deeply with them that they become a part of your identity. When you Create Space and raise your awareness of the rules you've adopted, you can decide if it's a rule that's serving you and whether you want to follow it. And when you do choose a rule, you can choose to hold it lightly, knowing it's a tool to help you take action, not to define who you are.

Reasons

We human beings are especially skilled at coming up with reasons to do something—or not do something. You can thank your mind, that great meaning-making machine, for that. It will come up with all sorts of reasons to avoid taking a risk or doing something new, because it wants to keep you safe. Entrepreneurs aren't immune to this, and we can come up with our own reasons not to start or move forward in our businesses:

- I can't start my own business. I don't have an MBA or any education in business.
- I'm way too disorganized/inexperienced/busy to do it.
- I might lose a lot of money if I start this business.
- I might fail.
- My family is notoriously bad at managing money, so I will be too.
- I'll move forward when the timing is perfect.

These are just a few I've heard from clients or experienced myself, and I'm willing to bet you could add a few more to the list. Are they true? Maybe, but maybe not. It might be true that you don't have an MBA—but how true is it that you can't start a business because of that? You might lose money starting a business—but how true is it that you could make a lot of money, too? You might fail—but you might succeed. (And that last one about waiting for the perfect time? Truth: There's never a perfect time to start.)

When you buy into the reasons your mind feeds you and believe they are true, that's Getting Hooked. These reasons feel true, and so we allow them to determine the action we take—or don't take—in our lives. But when you Create Space around these thoughts, you can look at them more objectively and choose whether you want to buy into them.

Judgments

If you take a close look at the examples of rules and reasons above, you'll notice something they have in common: Each contains an underlying judgment. For example:

> Rule: I can't start a business until I know exactly what I'm doing.
> Judgment: I don't know enough. Therefore I'm not good enough.

> Reason: I can't start my own business because I don't have an MBA.
> Judgment: I'm not smart enough. Therefore I'm not good enough.

There are other judgments that can cause entrepreneurs to struggle. Here are a few I've recognized in myself:
- I'm not strong enough to handle the stress of owning a business.
- People who sell things are sleazy, and I'm not going to be sleazy.
- I'm not well-connected enough to write a book or start a podcast.
- The coaching industry is filled with people who want to make a quick buck.

- There's nothing special about me that would set me apart from other therapists/coaches/consultants.

Making judgments is a part of our human nature, because we're wired to evaluate our environment and assess what's safe and what's not. There's nothing inherently bad about making judgments, but problems arise when our lack of awareness causes us to fuse with our judgments. When these judgments are unhelpful, they can hook us into thinking we're not good enough. It's like wearing blinders: All we can see is what our mind is telling us, and we don't see all of the available opportunities. Through the Create Space process, we can remove those blinders that limit our scope and expand our choices and options.

Past

Recently, an ad popped up on my Facebook feed for a webinar aimed at entrepreneurs looking to build their online business. Instantly, my face flushed, my heart rate quickened, and I became very uncomfortable. It had nothing to do the webinar, and everything to do with the fact that the last time I attended this person's online webinar, I bought the course she was selling—and never finished it. It's not that the course was bad (the few modules I completed were great) or that the course developer was out to take my money (quite the opposite; she had clearly put a lot of hard work, time, and energy into the project). Due to circumstances completely within my control, I simply failed to complete it. As a result, when I saw something having to do with this course, my default reaction was to remind myself of how I failed and convince myself that I just wasn't someone who could see things through to the end. Hello, shame spiral.

In retrospect, it's clear how this single 30-second Facebook ad led me straight down the path of Getting Hooked. I got caught up in a past mistake and allowed it to define me as a failure, as someone who doesn't follow through on commitments and therefore never will. When we get stuck in the past, consumed by failures, mistakes, hurts, wrongdoings, and wrong choices, we can become fused with those events. And this isn't limited to "bad" memories. We can also get stuck in our "glory days," reminiscing about how good our life used to be and longing to return to a better, simpler time. In both cases, Create Space can help us create separation between the thought and the self, so that our past actions don't have to define our present or future.

Future

Just as with the past, we can also Get Hooked by thoughts of the future. Whether we're worrying about what's to come or fantasizing about what else could be, the future offers all sorts of opportunities to fuse with our thoughts and Get Hooked. Here are just a few examples:

- You're working on a major presentation that you'll be delivering to a room full of your ideal clients next week. As you start to work on your next PowerPoint slide, an image forms in your mind: you, on stage, frozen. Hundreds of eyes are on you as you stand mouth agape, no words coming out. You stop typing and close your laptop. What if the presentation goes horribly wrong? You'll be humiliated.

- You're at a red light when you see a billboard for the state lottery. The projected winnings are in the millions, and you can't help but imagine what your life would be like if you won. You're already designing the living room in your waterfront mansion, where you'll interview potential board members for the non-profit organization you'll start. It's all so amazing— until the honking horn of the car behind you snaps you back to reality.

- It's 3 a.m. and you've been up for hours. Your mind is spinning as your mental to-do list grows longer and longer. There is just so much to do, and never enough time, money, or energy to get it all done. You're destined to fail before you even get started.

Although these are all hypothetical examples, if you're like most people, you likely had a reaction to one or more of them. That's how easy it is to Get Hooked. We can fuse with our perceived failures and flaws, even about things that haven't actually occurred. But just as with the past, Create Space can help us relate to our thoughts about the future differently, so that we can prepare and plan without overly attaching to the outcome.

Self

How you describe and relate to yourself is a significant area in which Getting Hooked occurs. Each one of us holds a concept of ourselves, and often this concept is rife with judgment. When we take time to reflect on how we view ourselves, we can uncover the ways we fuse our self-description with ourselves. What are some ways in which you might be Getting Hooked by your own self-concept? If you're like other entrepreneurs, maybe you've had some of these thoughts:

- I don't need a virtual assistant. I can do it all myself.
- I am so stressed out. I can't handle this anymore.
- That other designer/photographer/coach/blogger doesn't know what she's talking about. I'm right and she's wrong.
- I have no idea what I'm doing. I'm a total fraud.
- Without my business, I'm nothing. I'm worthless.
- I can't get professional pictures done until I lose weight/I gain weight/my skin clears up/I look better.

Each one of these examples reflects not only what the person is thinking, but how she views herself. And if she is super-fused with these thoughts, then they will significantly limit what she believes is possible in her business—and her life. But Create Space can help turn down the judgment dial, so that if and when these thoughts arise, their power is no longer automatic.

When to Create Space

Create Space is a process that can be practiced at anytime, any-where, for any number of reasons. In the last 24 hours alone, I relied on several Create Space techniques to help me when:

- I was stuck behind a slow driver in the left lane and angrily making judgments about them;

- My jeans felt tight and I berated myself for having that second cookie;
- I remembered a mistake I'd made in the past and felt the heat of shame wash over me;
- I woke up in the middle of the night, restless and overwhelmed by my growing to-do list;
- I got lost in a daydream about winning the lottery and my life magically changing overnight; and
- I failed to sign a prospective client and immediately questioned whether my business was viable and if I was cut out to be an entrepreneur.

In each of these situations, my mind generated all sorts of thoughts and my instinct was to buy into them: That driver is stupid and shouldn't be out on the road. I have no willpower when it comes to sugar. I'm never going to get everything done for my business. Who am I to write a book, and who on earth will want to read it? Thought after thought, judgment after judgment. It can really wear on me if I'm not careful. But instead of buying into each thought, I can Create Space around them using some the techniques described later in this chapter.

So here's the thing about Create Space: It's tempting to judge our success in practicing this process by how we feel afterward. If I feel less anxious, angry, or sad after, then it must have worked. If I don't, then I must have done it wrong. But that's not how it works. We don't Create Space to feel better; it's not about getting rid of thoughts or emotions, or reducing anxiety, depression, or other unwanted feelings. Instead, we Create Space specifically *for* those things. We allow those thoughts and feelings to come, to be, and to go, so that we can continue living our lives in a way that's consistent with our values. If we feel better during or after we Create Space, then that's a great secondary benefit—but it's not a guarantee, nor is it a marker of our success.

Okay, you might be sitting there, thinking, *Wait a second. I do all of this work, and I might not feel better after? I might feel the same, or even worse? Then what the hell is the point?* That's a fair question, so let's break it down a bit. First, it's important to notice the judgment inherent in the expectation of "If I do X, I will feel better." *Better* implies that you weren't okay or adequate to begin with—that there was something wrong. That's a judgment—a judgment you're buying into.

Second, the aim of Create Space isn't to manipulate your emotions. It's to increase your awareness of how your thoughts influence your behavior, and to empower you to take value-based action regardless. You can have the thought that you look fat in yoga pants, and still go to the gym and work out. You can feel anger toward your partner, and still show up for her important work event. You can even feel anxiety about your writing ability, and still sit down in front of the blank page and fill it. That's the benefit that comes from the Create Space process: You are moving forward in your life *alongside* whatever thoughts or feelings you have, not in spite of them.

But it Helps! And It's True!

Sometimes, a client tells me that Getting Hooked isn't a problem for him or her, and is instead helpful. The self-deprecating self-talk and anxiety about the future motivate them to try harder and do more. In fact, some of them are certain that their success is a direct result of the negative self-talk, and they don't know if they want to give it up.

If that's working for you, then far be it for me to tell you to stop. At the end of the day, every process, every technique, and every suggestion in this book is concerned with one thing, and one thing only: *workability*. How well is what you're doing working for you? How helpful are these thoughts and emotions in terms of achieving the success and happiness you want in your life? If your current strategy scores high on the workability scale, then you don't have to change anything you're doing. And if brow-beating yourself into action via a barrage of negative self-talk is how you want to achieve success, then more power to you.

But I don't want that for you. I don't want you to operate your business and live your life thinking that fear is the best—or only—motivator for success. Because it isn't, and there are so many other ways to achieve your ideal outcome that don't require you to insult or scare yourself into action. Russ Harris uses the metaphor of the rickety bicycle to address this belief. Negative self-talk is your rickety bicycle: It might get you where you want to go, but it won't be a very comfortable ride. Why take a rickety bicycle when you could walk, drive, fly, or ride a better bike instead? Create Space is the better bike—and I hope you'll give it a test ride before deciding to go back to the rickety bike.

Along the same lines, some clients have a hard time moving past the idea that what they're thinking is true. No matter how harsh the judgment, they are convinced that there's at least a kernel of truth in the thought, and because it's true, they have to believe it. But here's the real truth: It doesn't matter whether your thoughts are true or not. And I will never debate my clients about whether what they are thinking is true or not, because that's not what matters to me. What matters is workability. Is the thought helping you Determine What Matters and Make it So? Is it getting you what you want? Or is it a rickety bicycle?

TECHNIQUES TO CREATE SPACE

We've gone through what it means to Create Space, how it addresses the common pitfalls of its shadow process (Getting Hooked), and why Creating Space is of particular importance for entrepreneurs and small business owners. At this point in our tour of Create Space, it's time for our final stop: the techniques you can use to Create Space in your own mind and in your own life. As in the previous chapters addressing Determine What Matters and Make it So, what follows is just a sampling of defusion techniques available to you. I'm highlighting some that I have found particularly effective for both my clients and myself, and my hope is that you find them helpful too. However, this is not an exhaustive list, as a quick Google search of "ACT defusion techniques" will reveal. I encourage you to try one, a few, or all of the options that follow, but please know that if they don't resonate with you, there are others that might. (This would also be a great time to remind you that I love talking to my readers, and that you can email me at lee@caravelcoaching.com if you want to discuss other ways to Create Space.)

The techniques that follow come from the pioneers of Acceptance and Commitment Therapy, of mindfulness practitioners, and from the ACT community at large. As a therapist, coach, and human being, I have found ACT theorists and practitioners to be extraordinarily generous in sharing the tools they have created for their clients and themselves. In the spirit of sharing freely with others, I have modified some of these defusion techniques for my own personal and professional use, and I encourage you to do the same. Many are common practice in Acceptance and Commitment Therapy, and by using them, we are standing on the shoulders of those who came before us, and I'm grateful for their insight and generosity.

Thanks, Mind!

One of my favorite techniques to Create Space is called Thanking Your Mind, and it involves thanking your mind for its feedback. Created by Steven Hayes, the godfather of Acceptance and Commitment Therapy, it's used to reduce the emotional intensity of a thought by genuinely thanking the mind for that thought, with a sense of humor and true appreciation for its ability to attract your attention by any means possible.

In ACT, the technique of Thanking Your Mind is pretty simple. By saying thank you, you're detaching from the thought and seeing it as something separate from yourself. And that works fine, but being inquisitive and curious, I wanted to go a little deeper. *Why* am I thanking my mind? And why is my mind doing this in the first place?

So here's what I've come up with. As we discussed earlier in the book, our minds are incredible machines capable of creating extraordinary fantasies and possibilities for us. Sometimes these are pleasant, but often they aren't. Often, our mind harangues us with horrible thoughts and images of things that have happened in the past or haven't happened at all. It's like the mind is a safety monitor gone haywire. From an evolutionary perspective, the mind has developed to keep us safe. And thank goodness it has, because that's why our species survived.

But sometimes, the mind goes into overdrive. It is so concerned with our safety, it sends all sorts of messages intended to keep us stuck—and safe. Don't give that speech in front of hundreds of people; you might freeze or screw up and then people won't like you, and you won't be safe. Don't stop thinking about the time you got conned by a scammer; otherwise, it could happen again and you'll lose even more money, and you won't be safe. All of these memories and anxieties are there for one reason: to keep you safe. Sure, it's at the cost of your happiness and progress, but the mind isn't concerned with that. Its job isn't to make you happy. Its job is to keep you safe.

When you thank your mind, you are truly thanking it for its efforts in keeping you safe. It's done its job, and it's done it well. But now that you've detached from the thought, you can decide whether you need your mind to continue its role as safety monitor, or whether you'd like to delegate a different responsibility.

So the next time a distressing thought or memory or daydream comes up, try this simple script: "Thanks, mind, for that thought. I know you're trying to keep me safe, and I appreciate it. But because I don't need to be kept safe right now, I'm releasing you from that role. Instead, I could sure use your help in writing this book/talking to this client/designing this website." After a few times of thanking, releasing, and delegating, in the future all you'll need to say is "Thanks, mind!" and it will get the idea.

I'm Having the Thought That . . .

This is a quick and easy way to instantly Create Space between your thought and your identity. Choose any unhelpful, self-judging thought that your mind is feeding you. For example, maybe it's *I'm not smart enough to learn to code and design a website.* Get all caught up in that thought for a second, then take a breath and say to yourself, "I'm having the thought that I'm not smart enough to learn to code. . . ."

Sit with that for a moment, and then say to yourself, "I notice I'm having the thought that I'm not smart enough. . . ."

What do you notice happened? By adding those words to the beginning—*I'm having the thought that* and *I notice I'm having the thought that*—you are instantly and immediately separating yourself from the thought. You're not automatically internalizing the idea that you're not smart enough. Now it's an external, distinct thought, and you can choose whether or not to buy into it or reject it.

Bonus tip: This works really well with emotions too. The next time you have an unwanted emotion and catch yourself saying, "I'm sad" or "I'm angry," try saying "I'm having the feeling of sadness" or "I'm having the feeling of anger," followed by "I notice I'm having the feeling of. . . ." It may seem a little awkward at first, but it can de-escalate the intensity of the emotion, and it's a subtle reminder that you are not your emotions. You are so much more than how you feel.

How's that Working Out?

Sometimes, our thoughts try to seduce us with the notion of truth. If a thought is true, then I have to buy into it, right? Well, we've already talked about workability being more important than truth when it comes to our minds, and if that resonates with you, you'll love this technique.

The next time you have an unwanted or distressing thought that you judge to be true, ask yourself: If I go along with that thought and let it control me, where do I end up? What do I get as a result? How's that working out for me? What would it look like if I didn't buy into that thought, even though it might be true? Can I move forward anyway?

If you ask yourself these questions and are still facing a little resistance, that's okay. We're conditioned to believe that true is the most important thing, and so it might feel weird to discount a true thought. If that's your experience, I suggest digging a little deeper into the question: How's that working out? What thoughts, feelings, memories, or experiences does this thought help me avoid or escape from, at least in the short term? What benefits do I receive by adopting this thought and allowing it to take control? Am I willing to forgo the short-term benefits in order to move forward on my goal?

I've had to rely on this technique quite a bit while writing this book. One of the thoughts that I struggle with is *Who are you to write a book? No one will want to read it. You've never even published a book before.* There's a lot to unpack there, but part of it—not having published a book—is true. So some days, I'm able to acknowledge its truth and keep writing anyway, with the belief that someone, somewhere will read this book and find benefit in it. And other days . . . I let the thought control me. When I do, I get to avoid the uncomfortable experience of writing words down that I'm not sure are very good or that anyone will read. I escape the anxiety that comes from not knowing if this will be worth it in the end. And I get the pleasure of binge-watching the entire series of *The Office* on Netflix, even those awkward last two seasons. Once I acknowledge this, I can ask myself: Am I willing to experience the anxiety and discomfort that comes with writing in order to publish this book? What am I willing to have in order to get what I want? (If you're reading this book, then you know what I chose.)

Name It

One of my clients felt incredibly overwhelmed by everything that went into starting her psychotherapy practice. Between her licensure board, the state secretary of state's office, the county registrar, the insurance panels, the lease for her office, her own liability insurance—it was a mountain of paperwork. When she realized she'd submitted a form out of order and it was sent back to her with a denial letter, she burst into tears. "I am just so disorganized. And so stupid for not getting in right the first time. If I can't handle some simple forms, how will I manage my own therapy practice?"

After acknowledging her frustration and validating her anxiety, I asked her to list the thoughts and emotions that were coming up for her. I wrote them all down, and then asked her if we were to put all of these thoughts into a book or a movie, and it was called *The_____ Story*, what would she call it? She gave a small laugh through her tears and said, "Well, I guess it would be *The Stupid Sloppy Therapist Story*." So now, whenever any *I'm not good enough* thoughts come up about her practice, she says, "Oh look. There's *The Stupid Sloppy Therapist Story* again." She does so with equal parts humor and compassion, and in naming and calling out the story, she separates her sense of self from the story her mind is generating.

So the next time an unwanted thought comes up, notice it and name the story it's creating. Maybe it's *The Can't Please My Mother Story* or *The Never Going to Succeed Story*. Whatever you name it, see it as a story that your mind is creating—and a story you can choose to follow or not. By giving the story a name, you reduce its power and separate yourself from its narrative.

Mindfulness Meditation

In Chapter 2, we talked about mindfulness and how it promotes entrepreneurial flexibility. Sometimes, however, people hear the word *mindfulness* and they automatically equate it with meditation. Although I believe meditation is extraordinarily beneficial and is certainly relevant to our conversation, I want to stress that meditation is not the only path to mindfulness. I also don't want to imply that meditation is preferable to any other method. There are an endless number of ways to learn and practice the basic elements of mindfulness—separation, acceptance, present moment awareness, and observation—and what matters most is what will work best for you.

That being said, there are a few techniques in the ACT repertoire that are meditative in nature, and if you find benefit from practicing meditation, then these may be particularly helpful for you. The first is one of the original ACT defusion techniques developed by Steven Hayes and his colleagues, and it's called Leaves on a Stream. The second technique is an amalgamation of multiple guided meditations that I've practiced over the years that I call From All Sides, and it's particularly helpful in Creating Space from self-judgment. (Bonus: You can find recorded versions of these meditations at www. actonyourbusiness.com.)

Leaves on a Stream

1. Find a comfortable seated position, and allow your body to relax. Close your eyes, or, if you prefer, lower your gaze and allow your eyes to gently lose focus.

2. Imagine you're sitting underneath a large tree, on the bank of a gently flowing stream. This can be any kind of tree you want; it's your imagination. Allow the environment you create in your mind to be peaceful and relaxing. *(Pause 10 seconds.)*

3. As you sit under the tree, notice that every so often, a leaf gently falls from a branch and lands on the stream. The stream gently carries the leaf away, out of sight.

4. For the next few minutes, whenever a thought comes into your mind, place it on a leaf, and allow the leaf to fall into the stream and float away. It doesn't matter whether the thought is pleasant or painful, wanted or unwanted. Even if it's the loveliest thought ever, place it on a leaf and let it float by. *(Pause 10 seconds.)*

5. If you discover that your thoughts stop, simply focus on the stream. Eventually, your mind will start creating thoughts again. When it does, simply place the thought on a leaf and let it float away. *(Pause 20 seconds.)*

6. Let the stream flow at its own rate. You don't need to speed it up or slow it down. You don't need to wash the leaves away. Instead, you're allowing them to come and go in their own time. *(Pause 20 seconds.)*

7. If your mind tells you "This is stupid" or "This is impossible" or "I can't do it right," simply notice those thoughts and place them on a leaf. *(Pause 20 seconds.)*

8. If a leaf gets stuck, let it get stuck. Don't try to force it away. *(Pause 20 seconds.)*

9. If an unwanted or difficult emotion comes up, simply acknowledge it. If you feel bored, or anxious, or impatient, say to yourself, "Here's a feeling of anxiety" or "Here's a feeling of impatience." Then place those words on a leaf and let it float on.

10. From time to time, you may find yourself Getting Hooked by your thoughts and you'll forget about the exercise. That's a normal part of the process and will keep happening. Once you recognize you're Getting Hooked, simply acknowledge it and start again.

11. Continue placing your thoughts on leaves for as long as you wish. When you are done, you may bring the exercise to an end by sitting up in your chair and noticing what you hear, smell, or feel in the room. When you're ready, open your eyes.

After this exercise, you may notice that certain thoughts or feelings emerged repeatedly. Was it hard to let them go? Did you want to rush them away? What was it like to observe your thoughts in this way?

From All Sides

1. Find a comfortable seated position, and allow your body to relax. Close your eyes, or, if you prefer, lower your gaze and allow your eyes to gently lose focus.

2. Bring your attention to your breath. Notice what it feels like in your body as you breathe in and breathe out. *(Pause 20 seconds.)*

3. As you focus on your breath, you may find that a judgmental thought about yourself arises. When that happens, imagine that this judgment takes on a physical form. As you stand directly in front of it, what does it look like? Does it have a particular shape or color? What does it feel or smell like? *(Pause 20 seconds.)*

4. Imagine you are walking clockwise around it, and you are now looking at its profile from the 3 o'clock position. What do you notice about it from this perspective? What, if anything, has changed? Do you see anything beyond it? *(Pause 20 seconds.)*

5. Now continue walking around it so that you are directly behind it, at 6 o'clock. What does it look like from this angle? Do you notice anything new or different about it? What, if anything, do you see beyond it? *(Pause 20 seconds.)*

6. Continue to walk to the 9 o'clock position and view it from here. Has anything changed? What lies beyond it? *(Pause 20 seconds.)*

7. Now imagine that the form is hovering above you, and you are looking up at it. What do you see from this angle? *(Pause 20 seconds.)*

8. Now imagine that you are hovering above it, and you are looking down upon it. What can you notice about it from here? How does this view change your perception of it? *(Pause 20 seconds.)*

9. Now you are walking away from it. After a few moments, turn back and see it at a distance. What does it look like? What do you notice from this vantage point? *(Pause 20 seconds.)*

10. Bring your attention back to your breath. Notice the sensations in your body as you breathe in and breathe out. Slowly bring your attention back to the room, and gently wiggle your fingers and toes. When you're ready, open your eyes.

What was it like to give your self-judgment a form? In what ways did the form change based on your perspective? What was it like to observe your judgment in this way?

You can use other forms of guided meditation to help you observe your thoughts and Create Space from them, and you may find other metaphors to be helpful as well. Sometimes I imagine writing my thoughts in the sand and allowing the waves to wash them away. A client of mine prefers clouds in the sky to leaves in the stream. You could use grocery items on a conveyor belt, bubbles gliding (and popping) in the air, cars streaming by on a highway, or fish swimming by in the ocean. There is no right or wrong way to Create Space when it comes to visualization, as long as your focus is on releasing the thought and allowing it to come and go in its own time. The goal is not to force—simply to let be.

CHAPTER 10

Let it Be

WHAT IS LET IT BE?

If Create Space concerns itself with matters of the mind, then the process of Let it Be is all about the heart. In ACT language, this process is called Acceptance, and its importance in psychological flexibility cannot be understated: It's literally the "A" in ACT. Whereas in Create Space you separate yourself from your thoughts, in Let it Be, you separate yourself from your emotions. You give yourself permission to allow whatever emotions arise to be present, be they pleasant or painful. Rather than avoid or escape "negative" emotions, you make space for them and let them come and go as they will. Just as you allow your thoughts to come and go when you Create Space, you do the same with your emotions in Let it Be. You are letting your feelings be what they are, without allowing them to define or control you.

Acceptance is one of the most misunderstood concepts in terms of human behavior, yet it is such a critical component of psychological and entrepreneurial flexibility. But before I talk about what acceptance is, let me first talk about what it isn't. It is not about letting life happen to you. It's not passively allowing the difficulties of life to take you out and loving every minute of it. It's not about liking what happens to you, nor is it about forcing yourself to tolerate what you don't want.

Acceptance is simply taking objective stock of your emotional circumstances and acknowledging them. That's it. It's coming to terms with your present situation, and that includes your thoughts, your feelings, and your experiences. Practicing acceptance means you no longer avoid or try to get rid of your thoughts and feelings. Instead, you acknowledge them as a part of your current circumstances, allow them to be present, and move forward anyway. You Let it Be and Make it So. Notice that I didn't talk about Let it Be as resigning yourself to your situation. In this context, acceptance is about making space for our internal experiences—thoughts, memories, feelings, and so forth. It's not necessarily about the outside world, and it doesn't require you to let the world beat you up. In fact, ACT advocates the opposite: It calls for us to take meaningful action in the service of our values.

In fact, it is entirely possible to practice the Let it Be process while taking action. For example, let's say you have a friend who consistently talks about you behind your back and shares things you told her in confidence. (Side note: She's a shitty friend and you deserve better.) It's possible to practice acceptance (Let it Be) by acknowledging your thoughts and feelings (*I'm feeling hurt*, *She betrayed me*, *I'm so stupid*, *She's such a bitch*, and so forth), all while acting on your values (Determine What Matters) to either salvage the friendship or end it (Make it So). Acceptance is about approaching internal experiences without judgment and allowing them to be, all while taking action to live in alignment with what matters most to us.

Practicing true acceptance is hard work. When we first practice it, it feels unnatural to sit with unpleasant emotions and make room for them, which is understandable. Doing so feels unsafe, and that runs counter to all of the evolutionary-based tendencies we've developed to keep ourselves out of harm's way. That's why so many people unconsciously practice the shadow process of Running Away. Instead of meeting our feelings in the moment, we push them away, or distract ourselves, or simply refuse to acknowledge their presence. By Running Away, we provide a short-term solution to the problem of those pesky emotions—but in doing so, we create a larger problem of avoidance that can show up in other areas of our lives.

When you're able to stop Running Away and instead meet your feelings in the present moment, without judgment or expectation, then you're practicing the process of Let it Be. You're not only acknowledging the presence of those emotions, but you're allowing them to be there. There's no more trying to get rid of feelings or push through them. Instead, you're giving yourself permission to feel whatever it is you feel, and then returning to the task at hand. It's not about working your way through anxiety, pain, anger, or fear; it's more like working side by side with it. The rest of the chapter helps you uncover ways to sit with the feelings and Let it Be, while moving forward toward the business and life you want.

WHY IS LET IT BE IMPORTANT?

Let it Be and Create Space are the two core processes that are primarily responsible for creating mindset shifts. By acknowledging and working with (rather than against) unwanted thoughts and feelings, you develop greater resilience and mental flexibility, and you stop the pain-avoidance-explosion cycle in its tracks. Because the fact is, you can only keep those unwanted emotions at bay for so long before the hard work of suppressing them overwhelms you. Like a pressure cooker without a release valve, your emotions keep stewing and brewing until they eventually find a way out, often at the expense of other people and situations.

For example, let's say that you're feeling super stressed in your business. The work isn't coming in, your client leads are drying up, and you're anxiously wondering if you're going to be able to stay afloat. One of the clients you do have is driving you crazy with unreasonable demands that you feel like you have to meet, because you literally can't afford to lose them. Rather than acknowledge the anxiety and frustration, you shove them down and keep plowing ahead, so even though it feels like you're being productive, you're actually Running Away. No wonder when you get home that night and your partner forgets to put the dishes in the dishwasher after dinner, despite numerous reminders, you explode. All of the pent-up anger, frustration, anxiety, and fear come rushing out in a torrent of tears and yelling, and now on top of a floundering business, you feel like you're failing at your relationship, too.

Running Away is a seductive shadow process, because it feels like the right thing to do. If frustration, anxiety, fear, and doubt are keeping you from moving forward in your business, then powering through them to get ahead might seem like a good way to go. But trying to muscle your way through the pain only works for so long. Until those unpleasant, unwanted emotions are recognized, they will continue to stop you in your tracks, desperately trying to get your attention, no matter how hard you work or how focused you are. You've got to acknowledge and make space for them in order to move forward unencumbered. You have to Let it Be.

Now, before you accuse me of turning people into pain junkies who deeply explore every awful emotion, let me clarify something: Let it Be doesn't require us to accept every single thought or feeling, no matter what. Not only is that not realistic, it's cruel and detrimental to our emotional health. No, what I'm asking you to do is acknowledge when your unwanted feelings (and thoughts) are blocking you from moving forward in your life and keeping you from achieving your goals. If they are causing you to feel out of touch with your values and preventing you from taking positive action, that's when Let it Be comes in. In this example, the unwanted feelings of anxiety, frustration, and fear are blocking you from achieving what you want: a thriving business and a happy relationship with your partner.

What if, instead of allowing those emotions to fester and grow until they finally erupt, you were able to Let it Be? What if you could acknowledge the fear, the self-doubt, and the anger in the moment, and even allow them to inform your work instead of destroying it? What would be possible if those unwanted emotions didn't take you off-track? How much easier would it be to live a life consistent with your core values—and how much more pleasant would it be? That's what Let it Be offers. It's not about ripping off bandages or picking at old emotional wounds, nor is it about torturing yourself for the sake of wringing out every last drop of pain. It's about willingness—a willingness to experience whatever internal reaction is going on in the moment, whether desirable or not, because doing so is in alignment with your core values and deepest desires.

At the heart of ACT is the belief that acceptance is appropriate when it allows us to take action in line with our values. If these painful emotions are stymying your attempts to create positive momentum in your life, Let it Be is an appropriate tool. But this process is not about forcing you to confront every single emotion you experience. That would be exhausting—and counter-productive to taking action in your life. The point is to address the emotions that are getting in the way of creating and sustaining momentum in your life. If an emotion comes up that's not blocking you from reaching your goals in a fulfilling, adaptive way, then no need to force the Let it Be process. Just keep going.

The Experience Machine

In 1974, philosopher Robert Nozick created a thought experiment about pleasure and pain[8] that is definitely relevant to our discussion of unwanted emotions and Let it Be. In the experiment, Nozick asks us to imagine that scientists have created a great machine—the Experience Machine—that can give you any experience you wanted. No matter what you want (a successful business, a thriving marriage, the thrill of adventure), scientists could replicate that experience through this machine. Now, you wouldn't actually be doing these things. You'd be hooked up to the machine, floating in a tank with electrodes attached to you—kind of like a happier version of the precogs in *Minority Report*. But you wouldn't realize that. The machine would give you the sensations that you were actually having your desired experiences, and all the pleasure that comes from them.

So the million-dollar question: Would you plug into this machine for life, knowing you could have all of the experiences and feelings you wanted? Or would you pass? Would it surprise you to know that most people choose no, they wouldn't want to be hooked up to such a machine? It's true. Most people, when presented with this thought experiment, say they wouldn't choose to be hooked up because it wouldn't be a true reality. All your interactions would be a figment of your imagination, and your imagination would be controlled by the machine. And that feels creepy to most people (including me).

The unspoken part of this experiment, however, is that by choosing not to plug in, we are choosing to live a real, authentic life, even though it includes painful experiences and ones not of our choosing. We understand that part of what makes life extraordinary is the mix of experiences we have, including the distressing ones. In fact, perhaps the beautiful moments are made even more beautiful when compared to the sad or frustrating or tragic ones.

By turning down the Experience Machine, we are practicing Let it Be. We are making space for unwanted, uncomfortable emotions in the service of living a rich, full life. We inherently understand that pain is an inevitable part of life, a part we're willing to have in order to experience the beauty of life. In this, I'm reminded of the saying "Pain is inevitable, suffering is optional." By choosing not to plug in to the Experience Machine, we're willing to accept the inevitable pain. But practicing acceptance is about making suffering optional. The more we allow those feelings to be present, the less we suffer.

It's Not about Control

Let it Be counteracts a powerful force in human nature that ACT experts call Experiential Avoidance. This is another fancy term that means we try to get rid of, run away from, escape, or avoid unwanted thoughts, feelings, memories, sensations, and the like. Basically, if it doesn't feel good, we don't want it, whether it's in the real world or in our minds. And as I discussed in Chapter 5, this concept of Experiential Avoidance comes naturally to us because we're such great problem-solvers. If something is wrong, your mind works overtime to fix it, and this works great in the real world. Pothole in the road?

Walk around it. Scary saber-toothed tiger up ahead? Turn around and run away. Landlord doubling the rent for your office space? Find a new office. In these cases, Experiential Avoidance is helpful, because it keeps us safe and out of trouble. So naturally, the mind applies the same approach to unwanted emotions like fear, shame, anxiety, anger, and doubt. Because they don't feel good, that must indicate something is wrong, and your mind steps in to take care of it by avoiding it, successfully controlling the outcome.

Except unlike with the pothole or the tiger or the greedy landlord, avoidance doesn't work as well for internal experiences like thoughts and feelings. In fact, the more you try not to have a feeling, the more likely you are to have it, all while increasing your suffering. You might even argue that the bulk of suffering comes not from the emotion itself, but everything you do to try to avoid it. For some people, that avoidance shows up in the form of overindulgence, whether it be food, smoking, sex, alcohol, drugs, gambling—you get the idea. We run from our discomfort right into the arms of a quick fix, which feels great in the moment but not so much in the long run.

Some people use a more subtle form of avoidance, and focus all of their time and energy on other people. Why focus on my feelings when I can avoid them by getting lost in other people's worlds and helping them through it? Again, while this is an effective short-term solution (and more socially accepted than relying on a vice), it doesn't help for long.

That's why when it comes to Let it Be, the goal is not to control the emotion or how we experience it. You're not accepting an unwanted feeling in order to dictate how you experience it; that's not how it works. In fact, if your efforts at acceptance are aimed at reducing those uncomfortable feelings, then you're not practicing acceptance at all. You're merely *tolerating* the feelings, and that's a different action altogether. Even though you're not avoiding your feelings directly, you're still engaging in the struggle. You're still fighting against them as you try your best to get rid of them because deep down, it's not okay to feel them.

Let's say you have a client that grates on your last nerve. She's blunt, she's bossy, and you dread every interaction with her. Every time you complete a project, she comes back with nitpicky comments and demands a revision. She rarely expresses appreciation, and you'd fire her as a client except that she's well-connected in your field and, let's be honest, you could use the income.

It's tempting to say to yourself, "I really hate working for this woman, and I wish I could be done with her. But because I can't, I may as well deal with my frustration head-on and make the best of this. It's only temporary." On the surface, this looks like acceptance, right? You're not fighting against the emotion and you're not getting derailed from the task at hand.

Except . . . you're not really making space for the frustration. You're trying to rush through it and get the job done in order to reduce or get rid of it. And while that may be an effective strategy, it doesn't make for a pleasant experience. You'll be gritting your teeth through the process and hating every minute of it—and I'm willing to bet you didn't start a business so that you could be miserable doing it.

True acceptance means allowing those emotions to be present, just as they are. Much like with our thoughts and Create Space, Let it Be allows us to observe and detach from our emotions so that they don't have quite so much power over us. When we are able to Let it Be, we're able to meet these emotions from a neutral place, give them permission to be present, and continue on with our value-based actions.

So in the case of the client from hell, it means making room for frustration. It means turning to it and saying, "Hey, frustration. I'm definitely feeling you right now, and based on my previous experiences with this woman, it makes sense that you're here. So you're welcome to hang out for a while. Feel free to sit over there and do your thing. I'm going to get back to work." Don't laugh. I have had this very conversation in my head. And the result is that I no longer feel like I'm battling frustration or whatever emotion I'm feeling. Because the point isn't to get rid of it. I'm not struggling with it; I'm allowing it to be and redirecting my attention where I want it. Often the frustration dissipates, though sometimes not, and that's okay because it's not the point. The point is that struggle is over, and I'm able to reengage with my work in a way that feels good.

TECHNIQUES TO LET IT BE

We've reviewed what Let it Be is (and what it isn't), how it combats our tendency to stay safe by Running Away, and why entrepreneurs and small business owners benefit from practicing Let it Be. Now we're ready to explore how to actually Let it Be—how to make room for these unwanted feelings and get back to living in line with our values. There are so many ways to practice acceptance in your life, and this section covers just a few ways to do so. I encourage you to experiment and see what works best for you.

But first, an important caveat: If you have a history of trauma, then you may wish to consult with a mental health professional before engaging in these exercises. Many of the techniques I'm about to review have their roots in mindfulness practice, and there is nothing inherently unsafe or inappropriate about them. However, sitting with uncomfortable emotions is not easy, and for those of us with unresolved past trauma, it may trigger particularly difficult memories, feelings, and thoughts that are best explored with a therapist.[9]

In addition to the techniques in this section, you might find that the Create Space techniques described in Chapter 9 are useful to Let it Be. You can amend "I'm having the thought that . . ." to "I'm having the feeling that . . ." and notice what arises for you. Practicing "Name It" by naming the feeling and identifying the underlying story can also work in this context. And the two mindfulness exercises described in that chapter are also easily modified for use with feelings rather than thoughts. I encourage you to get creative and find what works for you. There's no wrong way to Let it Be.

Get Curious

The next time you notice a strong emotion come up, pause, take a breath, and get curious. Notice how the emotion surfaces in your body. Where in your body do you feel it the most? What sensations do you feel? Pretend you are a scientist or an explorer, and you're coming across this emotion for the first time. What words would you use to describe it? Are there any places where it feels different in your body than others? Any areas where it feels heavier or lighter? Sharper or fuzzier? Warmer or colder? Does it move or vibrate, or is it still? Pay close attention to the different ways the feeling manifests in your body, realizing that it may not be just one sensation; it may be a cluster of sensations, or layers of sensations.

Here's an example: The other day, someone I don't know posted in a Facebook group in which we both belong that she was looking for business coaching. I reached out privately to introduce myself and how I work with clients. One week later, she replied with a one-sentence response: "Thanks, but I'm looking for something a bit more advanced." *Gut. Punch.* Instantly, I felt ashamed, like I had been exposed as a worthless fraud and a terrible coach. Although my temptation was to shoot off a terse reply, I knew that would just be an avoidance tactic. Instead, I chose to put into practice everything I've been doing, teaching and writing about. I got curious.

I noticed that when I read her email, I literally felt shame rise within me, flowing up from my solar plexus and into my shoulders, neck, and head. My cheeks felt hot and tingly, and my throat constricted. Everything inside me felt like it was shrinking—my lungs, my heart, my stomach: all getting taken over by the intense, pulsing, heat of shame. I allowed myself to adopt the guise of a curious scientist, noting with impartial interest what was going on in my body. As everything shrank, I felt myself growing smaller and smaller. My non-scientist self felt like I didn't matter, like I was inconsequential, like I was dust. And the objective scientist in me simply noticed that response as well.

I stayed with the feeling of shame for several minutes—several long, very uncomfortable minutes. When I would get distracted by the perfect comeback or a revenge fantasy, I brought my attention back to the sensations in my body. And as I sat with shame, allowing it to be present, I noticed how the initial intensity softened, then receded. It didn't disappear altogether (and in fact, as I write this section, there's still some residual), but instead it pulled back from me, bit by bit. And the curious scientist noticed this, too: that once I passed a certain threshold, the shame stopped growing and instead contracted on itself, retreating.

Getting curious about my shame allowed me to practice acceptance and to Let it Be. I willingly sat with the discomfort of shame so that I could live in accordance with my values. Although it was incredibly tempting to shoot off a nasty email, that would not have been a value-based decision. Instead, by practicing acceptance, I acknowledged the emotion, made space for it, got curious about it, and let it run its course. Then I was able to get back on track and move forward in my business. (And if you're wondering if I replied, yes, I did, although it took me a few days. I suspected she didn't want a coach as much as a consultant, so I referred her to an excellent marketing strategist.)

Make Room

When an uncomfortable emotion makes itself known, our inclination is to try to avoid or escape it—and we know how that works out. So instead of trying to outrun it, make room for it.

As you feel the emotion come up, breathe deeply into it. If you'd like, close your eyes (or lower your gaze and allow your eyes to lose focus). Imagine your breath is able to permeate the feeling, going into, around, and through it. And as you breathe into it, your breath creates more space in your body and in your being for it. Imagine there's a gentle expansion that occurs around the feeling, allowing you to open up even more.

As you breathe into this feeling, you are giving it permission to be there. You don't have to do anything else except be present and allow it to be. If you notice a desire to get rid of the feeling, that's okay and perfectly normal. It's okay not to like the feeling, or how you feel. Just acknowledge that desire and remind yourself that you don't have to act on it. Just keep breathing into the feeling, creating space for it, and allowing it to be present. You're not trying to change it into anything else, although if it changes by itself, that's perfectly fine.

The goal of this exercise is not to "work through" or reduce any intense emotions. If the feeling changes or subsides, then great; that's a lovely secondary gain. But if it doesn't, that's okay, too. The practice is in the process of accepting the feeling in the moment, without struggling against it or trying to change it. You are making room for any and all emotions that come up, and you are demonstrating to yourself that no matter what emotion comes up, it is allowed to be there and you can make room for it.

Metaphors

One thing Acceptance and Commitment Therapy is known for is its use of metaphors to illustrate the core processes and key points. One metaphor that's particularly relevant for Let it Be is the quicksand metaphor.

Imagine you're hiking down a path, and you step into a patch of quicksand. Before you know it, you are falling deeper into the quicksand, and it's threatening to take you under. The more you try to escape it, the further down you sink. You try to jump, to run, to pull yourself up, but the quicksand pulls you further down with each movement.

Eventually, exhausted by the struggle, you stop. And in that moment, you realize that when you stop moving, you stop sinking. In order to survive, you have to stop moving and allow as much of the quicksand to come into contact with your body as possible. Rather than step up and down to try to outrun it, you have to do what feels counterintuitive: You have to lie down on your back, exposing your whole body to it, in order to free yourself from the quicksand.

Just as with quicksand, when you try and outrun anxiety, fear, anger, doubt, or any unwanted feeling, you inevitably find yourself slipping deeper and deeper into it. The more you try to escape, the harder the struggle becomes and the deeper you get. Instead, you have to willingly experience the feeling—just like lying back in quicksand. Only then does the struggle stop, allowing you to move through it.

If the quicksand metaphor doesn't resonate with you, perhaps the riptide metaphor will. Imagine it's a beautiful, sunny day at the beach, and you decide to take a swim. The ocean is calm, and you're enjoying the feeling of weightlessness as you float on the water.

Suddenly, you realize that the ocean has carried you farther from the shore that you want to be. Your feet can't touch the bottom, and you realize you're drifting farther out and you're caught in a riptide. Immediately, you start to swim toward the shore, frantically paddling, but it's not working. The current is pulling you out and you're getting exhausted.

Then you remember the signs on the beach: If you get stuck in a riptide, you have to swim parallel to the shore in order to escape it. It goes against every instinct, but instead of fighting the rip, you swim with it. You allow yourself to work with the rip, so that eventually you can get back to shore.

When we get caught up in emotions we don't want to feel, it's natural to try to fight them off and escape them. But this is the equivalent of swimming against the riptide; it's exhausting and counterproductive. The alternative is to acknowledge those feelings—to swim alongside them without struggle. Only then can we make it back to shore—back to our life.

The beauty of metaphors is that they can be anything that speaks to you. You are free to develop your own metaphor to describe the Let it Be process, and personalized metaphors are often much more powerful and meaningful. My hope is that the quicksand and riptide metaphors are helpful and that they inspire in you a new way of viewing the struggle.

Both Sides Now

This activity is particularly helpful when difficult emotions are making it difficult to move forward and take action.

On one side of an index card or a small piece of paper, write down the action you want to take and the values underneath the action. Be clear about what you want to do and why you want to do it. On the other side, write down the painful or difficult emotions that come up when you think about engaging in this action. If thoughts come up, that's fine; we can Create Space for them, too.

For the next week, carry this card or paper with you—in your backpack, your purse, your car, or any place where you can easily access it. When you start thinking about what you want to do, take out the card and ask yourself: Am I willing to have all of this—both sides now—or do I want to walk away? You cannot have just one side of the card. It's both or nothing.

I used this exercise with a client who was debating whether or not to make a major change in her business model. She had a very successful psychotherapy practice, but was considering transitioning to coaching full-time. Coaching felt more in alignment with her professional ideology and personal goals, but she was afraid to make the move. Some of her concerns were financial (Will I make enough money to sustain my lifestyle?) and others were more emotional (What will people think—what will my *clients* think—if I leave therapy behind?). Her index card looked like this:

Index Card	
Front of Card	**Back of Card**
I want to close down my therapy practice and start coaching full-time.	DOUBT: I'm giving up a profitable therapy practice and don't know if I'll make enough money.
I want to help women transition into midlife with grace and purpose.	ANXIETY: What will people think of me (negative thoughts about "life coaching")?
Doing so is consistent with my values of service, adventure, and love.	PAIN: I can't bear to hurt my clients' feelings or cause them to feel abandoned.
It will also allow me more flexibility and more time with my family.	FEAR: Do I really have what it takes to start a new business?

The point of this exercise was not to help her choose whether or not to close her therapy practice and start a coaching business (although eventually she reached to a decision). Rather, Both Sides Now is designed to help you experience the unpleasant, unwanted emotions in life and to willingly make room for them. Every decision has an emotional consequence, and it's futile to try to avoid them. Instead, ask yourself: What am I willing to have in order to get what I want? In my client's case, was she willing to have doubt, anxiety, pain, and fear in order to start a new coaching business? There isn't one right or wrong answer, but Both Sides Now allowed her to sit with the discomfort and Let it Be.

CHAPTER 11

Anchor Yourself

WHAT IS ANCHOR YOURSELF?

The fifth core process of entrepreneurial flexibility, Anchor Yourself, is a bit of an enigma, as it is both a separate process and part of the other five processes. ACT calls this Contact with the Present Moment, which is not only the name of the process but also a description of it. When you Anchor Yourself, you engage fully with the present moment so that you are aware of both your external experience, or everything going on in the world around you, as well as your internal experience, which includes your thoughts, feelings, and memories. It requires and builds your mental flexibility so that you can be fully conscious of both.

When we practice Anchor Yourself, we're getting at the very heart of mindfulness—how to be present and aware in the now. By keeping our focus on this moment, we are able to counteract our mind's chatter and mental static so that we can engage authentically and fully in our lives. This process is particularly helpful in moments when we feel overwhelmed, distracted, preoccupied, or disconnected, because it gently invites us to return to the moment and return to ourselves.

This all sounds great, doesn't it? Yet staying grounded in the present moment is another simple-but-not-easy task. As we've already discussed, the mind is really, really good at being our always-vigilant safety monitor, and it takes that job very seriously. No wonder it's easy to find ourselves lost in thought, ruminating about the past or worrying about the future. Anchor Yourself asks us to release the mind from its safety monitor role and recalibrate to the present moment, so that we can better assess what's happening now and how we should respond. Rather than replay an endless loop of what happened before or what's yet to come, mindfulness allows us not only to be here now, but to act here now as well.

There are many ways to Anchor Yourself, and I provide some specific techniques later in this chapter. However, there are three basic components to Anchoring Yourself:

1. Notice what's happening within and around you.
2. Allow your thoughts to come and go.
3. Allow your feelings to be present.

Do numbers two and three sound familiar? They should. They're Create Space and Let it Be. There's a symbiotic relationship between these processes, because they build upon and reinforce each other. Whether we are acknowledging and releasing our thoughts, or experiencing and making room for our emotions, both processes require an awareness of what we're thinking and feeling. Inherent in these two processes is self-awareness, which is at the core of Anchor Yourself. Separating from your thoughts and accepting your emotions are parts of being mindful, and being mindful increases your self-awareness. It's a cycle, and the more you practice them, the more natural it becomes.

But Anchor Yourself takes this a step further, because it means bringing your attention singularly to the present moment and being conscious of what's going on within *and* around you, without falling into the story of your thoughts and emotions. And that's very hard to do! In fact, as you practice, you might find that it's not long before your attention wavers and your focus wanes. Before you know it, a minute or two or 10 have gone by and you're out of the moment, having gotten sidetracked by a thought or invested in a feeling. You've unintentionally engaged in the shadow process of Time Traveling.

Essentially, there are three phases of time: the past, the present, and the future. Anchor Yourself is all about present moment awareness, so when you get caught up by your mind and pulled out of the present, then there are only two other places you can be (the past or the future). That's why I call the shadow process Time Traveling. When you're not living in the moment, you're either reflecting on the past or projecting into the future.

So here's the good news: If you're practicing mindfulness and you get distracted, you're normal and you haven't done anything wrong. In fact, by being aware of when you've lost the thread and bringing yourself back to the moment, you've done something right. Yes, the "present moment" part of this is important, but maybe even more important is the awareness aspect. It's natural for our mind to distract us with thoughts and feelings; it's how we're wired. But when you notice the moments when you get caught up by the meaning-making machine, you raise your awareness and strengthen your ability to be mindful. Getting distracted isn't a flaw; it's the very heart of practice. So when it happens, just go back to step one: notice it, and bring your attention back to the present.

Now, I don't want to suggest that it's inherently bad or wrong to spend some time in the past or future, because it's not. I treasure the memories I have of happy moments, and I love the thrill and anticipation that accompany looking forward to an exciting event. And even when we're dealing with unpleasantness, it can be helpful to reflect on past events and learn from them, or to plan for the future through mental preparation. However, given the mind's tendency to play the part of watchful safety monitor, we usually default into past or future thinking at the expense of the present. And when Time Traveling becomes our default, we miss out on what's happening in our world right now.

Instead, Anchor Yourself allows you to decide what is helpful and workable for you in the moment. By developing a practice of staying in the present moment, you'll be able to engage fully in your world and take actions that are consistent with who you are and what you want. For example, let's say you're meeting with a potential client, and your mind starts flooding you with memories of all the times you didn't nail your pitch and land the client. How helpful is that? In the moment, not very. But once you're aware of when and how your mind pulls you away, you regain the power of choice. You can either get caught up in those thoughts, or you can Anchor Yourself and connect with your potential client.

WHY IS ANCHOR YOURSELF IMPORTANT?

When it comes to entrepreneurial flexibility and the six core processes, I don't have a favorite. Sure, there may be one or two that I call upon more frequently, but all six are important to building a solid business and a fulfilling life. That being said, of the six core processes, Anchor Yourself is truly unique among the six core processes because it "anchors" the other five processes and entrepreneurial flexibility as a whole. Not only is it a separate process, but its emphasis on mindfulness is at the heart of the other five processes as well. Understanding Anchor Yourself is not only important for the purpose of an individual practice, but also as the framework for the entire concept of entrepreneurial flexibility.

When you Anchor Yourself, you engage in the practice of mindfulness to develop your awareness of what is happening in the moment, both externally and internally. Rather than automatically reacting to your circumstances, thoughts, or emotions, you're responding with intention. You're able to take in all sorts of information from the world around you, as well as your mind's perceptions and judgments, so that you can take purposeful action while remaining fully connected in and to the moment. You move away from feeling like life is happening to you, and instead you have more agency and control over how you show up in the moment. This power of choice is at the heart of entrepreneurial flexibility, and it's anchored in mindset, meaning, and mindfulness.

Mindset

Both Create Space and Let it Be are based in your awareness of your mindset and the messages your mind is sending you. When you Create Space, you're noticing the thoughts you're having without buying into them or getting enmeshed in them; you're simply allowing them to come and go. You're able to recognize them as part of your current circumstances, but you're not relying on them to define your world. Likewise, in Let it Be, when feelings and emotions emerge, you're observing them without getting entangled in them. They are a part of your present moment, but they don't determine or direct it.

Create Space and Let it Be require a high level of awareness about what's going on in the moment, and that's the very essence of Anchor Yourself. You're able to use mindfulness to observe your thoughts and feelings, and in observing your thoughts and feelings, you're becoming more mindful of yourself and your world. Practicing one process builds your ability to practice the other. And it works the same way with the shadow processes: When you fall into one, you fall into the other. Whether you're Getting Hooked by your thoughts or Running Away from your feelings, it's impossible to be present in the moment. You're too busy thinking about what might happen or what already happened. You're Time Traveling.

One of my clients described her experience this way:

> *Sometimes when I'm dealing with a client, I start worrying that things aren't going well or that my work isn't good enough. I replay things I could have said or done differently, or I start thinking about what my client might want next and mentally script my response. And then I realize I've missed what my client just said and I feel even more anxious and uncertain. I'm totally out of the moment.*

Did you notice how her thoughts and feelings pulled her out of being present for her client? How many times has that happened to you, where you've been so caught up in what might happen that you miss what's happening in front of you? No lie: This is a daily occurrence for me, and, embarrassingly, it happens most often with my husband or my kids. They'll be talking to me and I'll have no idea what they just said, because I've gotten distracted by a thought about work, or money, or my to-do list. I may be there physically, but I'm not there mentally. And although it's frustrating, there is a way to combat this. That's where Anchor Yourself comes in.

Meaning

It's not only the mindset processes that are interconnected with Anchor Yourself, but the meaning processes too. After all, the point is not to build self-knowledge simply for the sake of being more self-aware. We build our awareness so that we can engage with the world in a way connects us to our values, allowing us to live more fulfilling lives. And how do we that? By taking action that's consistent with who we are and what's important to us—or, in other words, by practicing Determine What Matters and Make it So.

In fact, when we merge present moment awareness with action, we heighten our sense of fulfillment and Make it So becomes an even more powerful process. We're fully engaged and connected with what we're doing, so the action we take is meaningful and purposeful. And yes, this is another simple-but-not-easy task, because it's so easy to resort to the default mode of living on autopilot, doing things not because they matter but for the sake of ease and convenience. Instead of being intentional in your choices, you're letting life happen to you, disconnected from your purpose and what matters most. You're deep in the shadow process of Losing Focus. And when you are unclear about your why, you'll find yourself trapped in a cycle of reactionary, escapist, or meaningless behavior—another shadow process, the Sisyphus Effect. To quote Russ Harris, "It's hard to act effectively when you don't pay attention to what you're doing."[10]

That's why Anchor Yourself is a critical component of bringing meaning and purpose into your life. When you are grounded in the present moment, you're better able to connect with who you are and what you want, and to take effective action. You're tapping into your highest self, aligning your thoughts, beliefs, and behaviors with your values. You're not just envisioning the business and life you want, but you're going one step further and actually creating it by taking action that supports your purpose. And it all starts with Anchor Yourself.

TECHNIQUES TO ANCHOR YOURSELF

At the heart of Anchor Yourself is mindfulness, which I described in Chapter 2 as paying attention to the moment with intention, purpose, and non-judgment. The good news about mindfulness is that there's no one way to do it, nor is there one right way to do it. Mindfulness is a personal experience, so you'll be able to create your own mindfulness practice based on what works best for you. In this section I introduce you to several different techniques that I encourage you to try, and even mix and match based on your setting, your mood, and your needs. Mindfulness can be fun and even playful, so don't be afraid to experiment a bit.

Focus on the Breath

Anchor Yourself requires you to be flexible with your attention, so that you're aware of both your outside and inside worlds. Because we're constantly bombarded with external stimuli through our senses, I like to start by orienting my focus inward and bringing my attention to my breathing. This technique is frequently used as both a meditation and a mindfulness practice, and it requires bringing your full attention to rest on the breath. When your attention starts to drift, simply notice the thought and return to the breath. You can do this for as long as you wish, whether for a minute, 10 minutes, or even longer.

If you'd like to use your breath work as a form of meditation, I've created the following script for you to use as a guide, and you can find a recorded version of it at https://www.actonyourbusiness.com. If you prefer, you can write your own guided meditation using this as a template. Again, there's no one right way to approach this. Just remember the three components of mindfulness: notice what's happening, Create Space, and Let it Be.

To begin, take a comfortable seated position and when you're ready, close your eyes or lower your gaze. Start by taking a slow deep breath, inhaling fully, and exhaling fully. Allow your forehead to be smooth and bring a soft, small smile to your lips. As your body relaxes, give yourself permission to let go of any stress or tension from the day.

Notice how the muscles in your neck and shoulders gently relax. You might find it helpful to imagine a thread attached to the crown of your head. That thread is gently pulling upward so that it creates space between your ears and your shoulders.

Now, direct your attention toward your breath. Notice what it feels like in your body as you breathe in and out. Feel the gentle expansion of your chest and your rib cage. Notice how your abdomen softly rises as you breathe in. And then, as you breathe out, how it gently collapses. The breath comes in, and the breath goes out.

Pay attention to the flow of your breath—how the air moves in through your nostrils, down the back of your throat, into your lungs. Then notice how it flows out. As you pay attention to the air moving in and out of your nostrils, notice the temperature, how it's slightly cooler as you draw the air in, and slightly warmer as you gently exhale it out.

As you continue to direct your focus toward your breath, allow your breathing to fall into a natural, comfortable rhythm. Notice where you feel the breath most strongly. Perhaps that's in your nostrils, or your rib cage, or your abdomen. Wherever you choose, maintain your attention on that area.

As you breathe, you might find yourself interrupted by a thought or a feeling. That's perfectly natural and part of the process. When you notice yourself becoming distracted, acknowledge the thought or the feeling, and then gently and compassionately return your focus to the area in your body where you feel the breath.

Devote your complete attention to the feeling of breathing in and breathing out. Continue to do this for as long as choose. And if a thought or feeling distracts you, simply notice it and redirect your attention back to your breath.

When you're ready, take a moment to check in with your body. Continue to breathe naturally, allowing yourself to remain fully relaxed. When you're ready, bring yourself back to the room and open your eyes.

This is one example of how to include breath work in mindfulness meditation. If you enjoy guided meditations such as this, you can find thousands of them with a simple Google search. Some of my favorites include Tara Brach's meditations (her Basic Meditations are a wonderful place to start), as well as Hay House Meditations, which you can download at whatever podcast player you prefer.

Sensory Activities

Rather than focusing on your breath and your internal experience, you can also practice mindfulness by directing your attention outward on your surroundings and bringing your senses into the experience. There are many ways to do so, but here are a few of my favorites.

Mindful M&M

This one is my interpretation of a classic Jon Kabat-Zinn exercise, Mindfully Eating a Raisin. In that classic exercise, you notice each and every aspect of a raisin as you place it on your tongue, keep it in your mouth, and eventually bite it. You notice every crevice and ridge as the raisin rolls over your tongue, and the slight sweetness and acidity as you bite into it. It might take you a full two or three minutes to mindfully eat that raisin.

To be honest, I don't like raisins that much. Golden raisins are fine, but your garden variety black raisin? No, thank you. Fortunately, you can practice this exercise with any type of food you want, and it just so happens that M&Ms are a great raisin substitute. Place a single M&M on your tongue, and notice the sensations that arise.

What does it feel like as the candy coating starts to melt away? Do you feel the graininess of the sugar, and then the translucent texture of the casing? Are there any rough edges to the casing as it melts? What happens when your tongue finally hits the chocolate? What does it feel like to bite into the M&M?

You can take this mindful eating perspective with you into your next meal. In fact, I challenge you to make the first bite of your next meal (or sip of your next drink) a mindful bite. What does it feel like as you bite into your sandwich? How would you describe the texture of the bread, the flavor of the roast beef, the crunch of the lettuce? What does it feel like as you take your first sip of coffee? Where do you taste it on your tongue, and how does it feel when you swallow and it glides down your esophagus into your stomach? See how long you can savor that first bite, and how it affects your appreciation of your food and of the moment.

5-4-3-2-1

The 5-4-3-2-1 mindfulness exercise is a great way to engage all of your senses. I suggest starting with a deep breath to center yourself, then notice five things you can see. This could be a car driving past your office, the dust on your computer screen, the brightly colored notepad in front of you—whatever is in your line of sight. Take your time with each item and really focus on the details. Perhaps there's someone in the backseat of that car passing your house, or maybe the smudges on your laptop screen form the shape of a heart. No detail is too small.

After you've examined five things using your sight, notice four things you can hear. Even in a quiet setting, you can probably pick out four things. Perhaps it's the hum of the refrigerator, the sound of the air conditioning unit cycling on, or a bird chirping outside. Again, just as you did with your sight, notice every little detail of the sounds you hear. Is there a repeating cycle to the refrigerator hum? Does the bird call change in length or tune?

Repeat this process with three things you can touch, two things you can smell, and one thing you can taste. With each sense, you are closely attending to the experience. Maybe you feel the contrast between the softness of your leggings, the slight scratchiness of your sweater, and the weight of your shoes. Can you smell the coffee you brewed this morning, or maybe the perfume of a coworker? What do you taste in your mouth? Take your time with this, and savor every sensation. Just as with the breath work, you're devoting your complete attention to your experience and grounding yourself in the present moment.

Do the Dishes

Confession time. I learned to cook so that I wouldn't have to do the dishes. We have a rule in our house that whoever cooks doesn't have to clean up, so I got really good at cooking. But here's the problem: My husband believes that leaving a pot to soak overnight is necessary, and inevitably I wind up cleaning it the next morning. Now, I know one dirty pot isn't really that big of a deal. And my husband is a wonderful, hardworking, generous man. But even knowing all of those things, I'd still find myself getting angry and resentful about having to clean the pot.

Then one morning, I tried something new. Inspired by Gretchen Rubin's mantra, "If you can't get out of it, get into it," I decided to conduct an experiment. What would it be like to mindfully wash this pot? I turned on the water and felt my nerves fire as the temperature changed from cold, to warm, to hot. I inhaled the aroma of the dish soap, noticing the subtle note of lavender underneath the predominantly soapy scent. I felt the soap bubbles pop gently against my skin as the rough edges of the scrubber scraped against the residue in the pot. For two full minutes, I scrubbed that pot with my complete attention. Sometimes I would get bored, or resentful, and I would just notice the feeling and return my attention to my task. And when it was done, I noticed the softness of the dish towel and the smoothness of the pot as I ran the cloth over to dry it.

When we bring our full focus to the present moment, we bring an appreciation and perhaps a reverence to even the most mundane task. The next time you have a chore to do—maybe it's vacuuming your office, or taking out the trash, or, yes, doing the dishes—bring a little mindfulness to it and see what happens.

(For the record, I still don't enjoy doing the dishes. But I mind the chore much less when I do it mindfully.)

Drop Anchor

Russ Harris coined the term *Drop Anchor* to describe a simple centering exercise, and it's the inspiration behind Anchor Yourself. You can Drop Anchor any time you want, but it's especially helpful when you feel yourself Getting Hooked or Running Away.

Start by planting your feet firmly on the floor. As you push them down, notice how the floor is supporting you. Notice how your muscles flex and tense as you continue to push down. Pay attention to the force of gravity on your body—how it gently pulls your head, neck, shoulders, spine, and legs toward the earth. Once you are firmly anchored, return your attention to the world around you. Use your senses to engage in the world around you. Notice what you see, hear, touch, smell, and taste. Now notice where you are, and return your attention to the task at hand.

Mindful Moment

If meditation isn't your thing, then try incorporating a Mindful Moment into your day. This is a technique I use whenever I'm feeling bored, impatient, unfocused, or anxious. When I notice the feeling, I stop and take a mindful breath. Just as I described in Focus on the Breath, I pay attention to the physical sensations of the breath entering and exiting my body. I might do this for one breath, or five, or 10 (however long I need in the moment).

You can use this technique any time you want, and it can be a spontaneous choice or something planned. For example, there are certain events in my day that I've set as triggers for a Mindful Moment. When I'm stopped at a red light—Mindful Moment. I focus on my breathing until the light turns green. When I'm about to start a phone call with a client—Mindful Moment. I take several deep, engaged breaths before our session begins.

My favorite and most random Mindful Moment is whenever I refill the water compartment for my espresso machine. When my family moved back to the States from Germany, I came home with a serious penchant for good espresso. In order to feed the beast, I bought a DeLonghi espresso machine, and it gets serious use in my house. The water compartment holds about 56 ounces of water, and it takes about a minute to fill it using the filtered water tap on my refrigerator. So every time I refill the compartment—Mindful Moment. It takes about five or six deep, focused breaths to fill it up, and when I'm done, I'm ready to go.

Although I normally Focus on the Breath as part of my Mindful Moment, you don't have to limit yourself to breath work. You can do just about anything as part of your Mindful Moment, provided you are paying full attention to the moment with intention, purpose, and non-judgment. For example, I'm writing this section at my dining room table, in front of a window that overlooks my front yard. Whenever I feel stuck in my writing process, I look up and take a Mindful Moment.

Right now, I'm noticing how the branches of the bush in front of the window sway in the wind, and how one is bending ever so slightly under the weight of a bee that has landed on it. I see the silhouette of the tree against the sky, noticing the vibrant green against the bold blue, and how the branches are now covered with leaves when only a few weeks ago they were barren. I hear the call of the mourning dove, my favorite bird, and I'm pulled back to when I was a kid, when I could hear mourning doves from my bedroom. Then I catch myself Getting Hooked by a memory, so I return my attention to the present and on what I see before me. With a greater sense of focus and calm, I return to my writing.

Catch Yourself

Often, the behaviors that we most wish to change are driven by Getting Hooked and Running Away. They can be addictive behaviors, such as drinking, disordered eating, gambling, sex, and so forth, or seemingly benign actions, like, oh, I don't know, maybe binge-watching all nine seasons of *The Office* instead of finishing the next chapter of your book. Regardless of where they fall on the spectrum, each of these activities is a way for us to avoid dealing with unwanted thoughts, uncomfortable emotions, or unpleasant activities.

So the next time you catch yourself about to engage in a fear-based or avoidant behavior, pause for a moment. Take a deep breath, and have a Mindful Moment. What sensations are going on in your body? What thoughts is your mind producing? What feelings are coming up? Are you trying to push any of them away? What is your mind telling you to do or believe? When we engage mindfully before we take that next step, we are more likely to move away from autopilot or self-sabotage, and toward behaviors that are in line with our values.

And sometimes, we don't catch ourselves in time. We're halfway through a can of Pringles or a bottle of wine, or zoned out in front of the television. So if you don't catch yourself before, catch yourself during. Observe what's going on for you as you engage in whatever unwanted behavior you're doing. Notice every aspect. What's the texture of that Pringle? Where do you taste the salt on your tongue? How does that couch cushion feel against your skin? Really dive in and get present, and see what happens. Sometimes, simply meeting the present moment with full attention and awareness is enough to disengage and get back on track.

CHAPTER 12

Observe Yourself

WHAT IS OBSERVE YOURSELF?

The sixth and final process of entrepreneurial flexibility is Observe Yourself, or what ACT refers to as Self-as-Context. I get that this process might sound a little woo-woo at first, but bear with me, because I believe Observe Yourself is the secret to true happiness and fulfillment. Observe Yourself teaches us how to mindfully show up in our businesses, our relationships, and our world, and it's rooted in the incredible capacity we humans have to create, engage in, and notice an experience—all at once.

Before I dive in to the theory behind Observe Yourself, it might be helpful to start with an example. Recently, my youngest son, Ben, asked me to snuggle with him before bed. This was a big deal, because Ben is 9 going on 19 and not really into parental displays of affection. So there he was, Mr. Too Cool, asking me to tuck him in and snuggle. And you better believe I did.

While we were snuggling, I had this moment. I was watching him breathe and I thought to myself, *Wow. This moment is happening right now, and I'm here for it.* I was present with my son, and I was aware I was with him. I was creating and having an experience with him, and

I was fully aware that I was having the experience. That is Observe Yourself in action.

When we are able to take a step back and truly notice our experiences, then we're tapping into our power of observation. I go into this idea and the concept of the Observer Self in this chapter, but for now, just know that this type of meta-level observation is one aspect of mindfulness. When we are grounded in the present moment, accepting our internal experiences, and not enmeshed with our thoughts, we can tap into this higher observation. And we can do it anytime we want.

The Three Selves

Did you know you're actually made up of three selves? I'm not talking about split personalities; I'm talking about three different perspectives from which we view the world. When you understand each of the three selves, it becomes easier to understand what Observe Yourself is all about, and which perspective you're taking on life.

The first self is what ACT calls the conceptualized self or Self-as-Concept. I prefer to think of it as the first level of self, or the Thinking Self. This self contains all of the things we normally associate with what makes you *you*—all of the thoughts, feelings, beliefs, facts, judgments, experiences, and stuff that goes into your view of yourself. If someone were to ask, "Who are you?" most of us would probably answer from this level of self: I'm an entrepreneur, I'm smart, I'm a parent, I'm short, I'm American, and so forth. Although some of the conceptualized self is based on external factors, our view of ourselves from this perspective is largely influenced by our internal experience—all of that mindset stuff we explored in Create Space and Let it Be.

The second self is something we just explored in the previous chapter, and is what ACT calls Self-as-Awareness. I like to think of this level as the Being Self. From this perspective, you are what you tap into when you Anchor Yourself. You are the ongoing process of noticing and contacting the present moment, and you are becoming increasingly self-aware of yourself and your surroundings. You don't define yourself by what you think or what you do. At this level, the focus is on being. The answer to "Who are you?" is simply "I am."

As you become increasingly aware, you're able to access the third self, which in ACT language is Self-as-Context, or the Observer Self. The Observer Self is the space from which you notice yourself, or the viewpoint from which the noticing occurs. It is the part of you that is always aware, noticing what's going on in any moment, and this is the self you access when you practice the process of Observe Yourself.

This part gets a little tricky to describe because the notion of the Observer Self doesn't lend itself to words very well. Words are the domain of the Thinking Self, because all of those words create thoughts, images, facts, and judgments to help us interpret and make sense of the world around us. The Observer Self has little use for words because it's not focused on interpreting and processing—it is simply noticing—which is why it's hard to use words to describe the process. Despite the limitations of language, metaphors can be an effective way to communicate these transcendent concepts, and the Self-as-Sky metaphor, with its roots in eastern philosophy, is a lovely description of the Observer Self:

> *Think of the sky as your Observer Self. The sky is always there, always present. Your thoughts, feelings, memories, judgments—all of your mind's creations—are the weather. The weather is constantly changing—one day it's sunny and warm, the next may be stormy and dark—and yet the weather has no effect on the sky. No matter how terrible the weather, it does not harm the sky. Violent thunderstorms, terrible blizzards, hurricanes, and tornados—they do not change the sky. In fact, the sky has room for all kinds of weather, always.*

> *During tumultuous weather, we might not be able see the sky, as it is blocked by clouds. But even though we can't see the sky, it is still there. And when we rise above the clouds, eventually we return to the same, constant sky. It is always there.*

I was reminded of this metaphor not too long ago, while flying home from a conference in bad weather. Sitting on the plane, watching the rain stream down the window and noticing the ominous clouds, I wondered if it was safe to fly. Clearly, I wasn't the only one worried, as the pilot came on and assured us that, although it was raining, there was no lightning and we were clear for takeoff.

As the plane headed down the runway and gained speed, I had a moment of panic. My mind was creating all of these devastating scenarios: the plane skidding off the runway or getting struck by an errant unseen lightning bolt and falling from the sky. Talk about a "Thanks, mind!" moment. And when we first became airborne, the turbulence was extraordinary. I'm not usually a nervous flyer, but in that moment, I was scared.

And then, as we broke through the thick layer of clouds and ascended higher and higher into the sky, the foreboding darkness disappeared. We were greeted by the blue sky, and the sun created a golden silhouette behind the clouds before emerging in its full glory. We entered the atmosphere in peace, leaving behind all trace of storms and fear.

The storms on the ground felt so real—so scary—and they were all my conscious mind could comprehend. But those clouds masked a deeper, peaceful sky that was also there and just as real. The sky had never abandoned me; I just wasn't conscious of it.

When you transcend the clouds and emerge into the sky, you're able to view yourself and your world from a different plane (so to speak). You are aware of what you're thinking, feeling, and doing as you are thinking, feeling, and doing it, and you do so without judgment. That's the power of Observe Yourself, and it will radically change how you approach your life.

WHY IS OBSERVE YOURSELF IMPORTANT?

Although Observe Yourself can feel almost spiritual in approach, it's not about getting meta just for the sake of getting meta. The application of Observe Yourself can lead to benefit in the real world, including in your business. I have no doubt that the positive effects are endless, but I've observed four key benefits when coaching my clients: reducing overwhelm, developing clarity, uncovering purpose, and increasing self-acceptance. Let's take a quick look at each of those aspects and how they can support your business growth.

Reducing Overwhelm

I've noticed a pattern emerge in some of my clients (and in myself, too) when it comes to feeling overwhelmed in their businesses. Although the details differ from person to person, the process looks similar and consists of three phases:

- Phase One: An idea—a really, really good idea—forms. That idea starts to expand and grow into an incredible vision of what could be—what will be. The energy is electric and everything is exciting. The possibilities are endless.
- Phase Two: Work begins. The vision starts to come to life.
- Phase Three: Panic sets in. What once was brilliant is now irrelevant, boring, and/or terrifying. The thought of continuing to work on the vision is completely overwhelming. Energy plummets, self-doubt rises, and panic leads to helplessness and even burnout—until the next idea comes along and the cycle repeats.

I know this territory all too well. The Land of Opportunity and the Land of Overwhelm share a border that innovators and creators often straddle. It's a no-(wo)man's-land where ideas dissolve and creativity languishes if we stay too long. So how can you navigate your way out of the border zone—or bypass the border zone altogether? Through the process of Observe Yourself.

At each phase, you can utilize Observe Yourself to notice what's going on. Admittedly, this is easier to do during the first two phases. In the first phase, you're engaged with the energy of a new idea, but you're also able to maintain a detached, objective perspective. You're fully present without becoming enmeshed with the idea. Similarly, in the second phase, you are Observing Yourself bringing this idea to life. You are creating, experiencing, and observing each detail from a place of interested detachment.

In the third phase, it can be more difficult to engage in the Observe Yourself process. You're on the verge of allowing the overwhelm to push you under, and you may feel like you don't have a choice. But you do. You always have a choice. You can Observe Yourself. Notice that you are having the feeling of overwhelm. Train your awareness on how that overwhelm is showing up in your body—how it's unlocking your mind's tendencies to create unhelpful stories. When we notice without judgment, we turn down the intensity dial and are able to see clearly what's really going on.

No matter what's going on, Observe Yourself allows you to create a safe, neutral place from which to respond. No matter how unpleasant the thought or feeling, there is always a safe space inside from which we can practice the meaning and mindset processes and choose our response.

Developing Clarity

When I first started my coaching business, I was excited to get out there and change the world, and I had all sorts of ideas how to do it. I could start a coaching group! I could hold a retreat! I could create a course! I could work with women! Or helping professionals! Or creative entrepreneurs! Or just keep it to therapists! So many possibilities; what to choose?

There I was, stuck in the border zone between the Land of Opportunity and the Land of Overwhelm, completely unsure what to do next. Not only was I overwhelmed, but I was confused and disoriented, and the more I thought about what my next step should be, the more uncertain I became. I sensed myself losing momentum and starting to get stuck.

When we feel overwhelmed, it's often accompanied by a sense of uncertainty or disconnection. So if Observe Yourself can help reduce feelings of overwhelm as I described above, then it makes sense that it also directly addresses any confusion that comes along with it. From this detached, objective perspective, we notice the cause of our ambivalence and how we may be contributing to it. With that insight, we're able to cut through the confusion and gain greater clarity.

In my case, Observe Yourself allowed me to take a step back and identify what was really going on. I noticed that in my sincere desire to serve others, I was also getting wrapped up in doing everything right, right now. My perfection and my impatience were contributing to my overwhelm, and I was getting in my own way. I needed to make the perfect choice, create and implement a perfect program, and get it all done—yesterday. By holding myself to an unrealistic standard, I was sabotaging my efforts before I'd even begun. No wonder I felt overwhelmed and confused!

By stepping back and observing, I gave myself the gift of clarity about how perfectionism and impatience can derail a business, and why it's important to temper the energy of opportunity with objectivity. Moreover, I also gained clarity about the next steps in my business—not just the action I would take, but the energy I wanted to bring into my work. Observe Yourself allows you to take a 30,000-foot view of yourself and your world so that you can see what's really going on, and, instead of judging it, you can take action.

Uncovering Purpose

On any given day, we make thousands of decisions. This morning alone, I decided whether to get up with my alarm or hit the snooze button, whether to brush my teeth before or after my shower, whether to go with the cute skirt or my favorite jeans—all that just in the first five minutes I was awake. And yet for all of them, the decision didn't feel like a choice. I hit the snooze button because I always hit it once (and set my alarm early to do so). I brushed my teeth before the shower because that's what I always do. And I went with my jeans because I could hear my kids calling me and my jeans were within reach.

The decisions I made this morning had something in common: I made each from a default state. I chose the snooze button and the before-shower tooth brushing because they're habitual. I chose the jeans because I was under stress and defaulted to the easiest option. When we make decisions from a default state, we're not always conscious of what we're doing, and we're certainly not aware of why we're doing it.

This isn't necessarily a big deal when it comes to getting ready in the morning, but it can be a *huge* deal when it comes to operating your business. When our default is to do what we've always done simply because we've always done it, we lose track of our why. And when we're out of touch with our why, we find ourselves back in the shadow process of Losing Focus.

When I started my business, even though I was creating a brand-new coaching practice, I brought with me two old friends: perfectionism and impatience. Under stress, I defaulted to feeling anxious and over-whelmed because nothing seemed good enough and I wasn't making progress quickly enough. Only when I slowed down and practiced Observe Yourself was I able to recognize how my default state was influencing my decision-making process. And that led me to ask a very important question: *What the hell am I doing?*

Put another way, I paired Observe Yourself with the mean-ing-based processes of Determine What Matters and Make it So to reconnect with my *why*. Why did I start Caravel Coaching in the first place? Because I want to serve other helping and healing profession-als as they build businesses they love. I want to increase connection and reduce isolation among entrepreneurs and small business owners. I want to strengthen my profession and my community through meaning, mindset, and mindfulness. And I can do that through coaching, through speaking, through writing, and through connecting others.

Developing clarity and uncovering purpose go hand in hand, and are two extraordinarily powerful results of Observe Yourself. By viewing yourself and your world objectively, and by noticing how you create, participate in, and observe your life all at once, you create a space in which you can access your deepest wisdom and discover what matters most.

Increasing Self-Acceptance

In a world that focuses on getting more, doing more, being more, the idea of self-acceptance can feel both aspirational and unattainable. It's tempting to think that we're just one job, one diet, or one relationship away from being happy and feeling like we're enough. And yet even if we score the perfect job, lose those last 10 pounds, or meet the person of our dreams, there's still a void that's rooted in a belief that we're not good enough the way we are.

But when you invoke the process of Observe Yourself, you're able to transcend that "not enough-ness." You can enter that safe space from which you notice what's going on without attaching to it, and you can call on the other core processes to support you. You might Create Space around the thought that everything will be better once you land that promotion. You could notice the feelings of sadness and loneliness that accompany your desire to weigh less, and Let it Be. You might catch yourself daydreaming about Mr. or Ms. Right and how your life will miraculously improve once you're in a committed relationship, and choose to Anchor Yourself. All of these processes are complete on their own, but when paired with Observe Yourself, you go beyond the action implicit in each process and notice your role in creating, experiencing, and observing the action.

But the key to Observe Yourself isn't simply in noticing or paying attention. It's doing so objectively and without judgment. When you enter that space of observation, you transcend the impulse to evaluate the things, events, or people in your life—including yourself. You approach your life with a neutrality and an understanding that things are not inherently good or bad; they just are. When you strip away the judgment, you create the opportunity for self-acceptance.

One of my coaching clients experienced a powerful shift into compassion through the process of Observe Yourself. She started seeing me because she had a history of starting projects and not finishing them, which was adversely affecting her business. She had a long list of business-building strategies—workshop topics, blog post ideas, a podcast concept, a book proposal—all of which she had abandoned early in development. She was incredibly frustrated with herself and feared she was destined to suffer from shiny object syndrome forever.

During one of our coaching sessions, I led her through a visualization exercise in order to practice Observe Yourself (an exercise I share with you later in this chapter). During the exercise, she saw herself not as a bumbling business owner who couldn't follow through on things, but as a talented young woman re-creating a cycle she had learned in childhood. She saw herself as a little girl who craved the love of a disconnected parent and who would take on new endeavors to gain her parent's attention. Occasionally she was rewarded with approval, but more often she wasn't. And when she "failed," she stopped what she was doing and tried something new.

Through Observe Yourself, she saw how and why she was creating and sustaining this cycle, and, instead of judging or berating herself, she met herself with understanding. It made sense she would have difficulty following through on things, because she had trained herself to move on if something didn't succeed quickly. With this revelation, she was able to grant herself compassion and love, and her relationship with her business shifted.

TECHNIQUES TO OBSERVE YOURSELF

When it comes to putting the process into practice, Observe Yourself is unique. With the other five processes, there are clear-cut, easy-to-implement exercises that I can walk you through, each with their own identifiable outcome. With Determine What Matters, you're aware of your values, and with Make it So, you've got an action plan. With Create Space and Let it Be, you're creating distance between yourself and your thoughts and emotions, respectively, so that you've got space to implement your Make it So action plan. Even with Anchor Yourself, there are specific actions you're taking to incorporate mindful living into your day-to-day routine.

But Observe Yourself is a different beast altogether, because it boils down to one instruction: notice yourself noticing. And you can do that for anything you do, including the other five core processes. As you Determine What Matters, notice your awareness of yourself and your values. As you Create Space, notice yourself as you separate from your thoughts. As you Anchor Yourself, notice who is paying attention to each in-breath and out-breath.

In fact, you can add Observe Yourself to just about any Anchor Yourself exercise simply by adding the instruction to "notice who is noticing." Any mindfulness exercise can become an opportunity to Observe Yourself. And why stop there? Any action you take can be an opportunity to Observe Yourself. All you have to do is pause and notice the noticer, the Observer Self. For example, the next time you sip your coffee, you're noticing where on your tongue you register its taste, you're noticing how it feels as you swallow and warms the back of your throat and goes into your stomach—and you're noticing who is doing the noticing. Or as Russ Harris puts it in *Act Made Simple*, "the 'you' behind your eyes who is noticing all this."[11]

As with all of the core processes, Observe Yourself is—wait for it—simple but not easy. It's simple to notice yourself noticing, but to do so requires the ability to view yourself objectively, without judgment, and in the present moment. And given that we human beings are evolutionarily designed to judge, plan for the future, and analyze the past, that's hard to do! It takes practice, and part of the practice is noticing when you fall back into judgment—and then noticing who noticed the fall.

In time, Observing Yourself will feel second nature, but to help facilitate the process, I'm including two mindfulness exercises that can help you tap into the Observer Self. You Are Constant is based on a classic exercise by Steven Hayes, the creator of ACT, and his colleagues. Your Personal Theater is adapted from several exercises shared within the ACT and coaching communities, and I encourage you to adapt it for your use as well. You can find recordings of both of these exercises at https://www.actonyourbusiness.com.

You Are Constant

The following exercise has been adapted from the seminal observer exercise developed by Steven Hayes for the original ACT protocol. At the heart, it consists of four steps:

1. Notice X.
2. There is X, and there is you noticing X.
3. If you can notice X, you cannot be X.
4. X always changes. The you who notices X is constant.

X may be anything you want it to be. X can be your breath, your body, your thoughts, your emotions, the actions you take, the roles you assume. What you choose as X isn't important. The key is recognizing you are noticing X, and therefore are not X, and that you remain constant. Here's a script to walk you through this process:

To begin, take a comfortable seated position and, when you're ready, close your eyes or lower your gaze.

Start by taking a slow deep breath, inhaling fully, and exhaling fully. Notice the breath as it moves in and out of your lungs. Notice the air as it flows in through your nostrils . . . into your lungs . . . and out again.

As you do so, be aware that you are noticing. Here is your breath, and here you are, noticing it. This is the process of Observe Yourself.

If you can observe your breath, then you cannot be your breath. . . . You are not your breath.

Notice how your breath changes. . . . Perhaps it started out shallow and deepened as you relaxed. Perhaps you're now breathing slower than you did before. . . . Your breath has changed . . . but the part of you that notices your breath has not.

You have been breathing your entire life. Your breath has always changed. When you were a child, your lungs were smaller . . . but the you who could notice your breathing as a child is the same you who notices it now as an adult. You are constant.

You might find that your mind is debating, analyzing, or critiquing. . . . That's perfectly fine. So now, pause and observe your thoughts. Where are they? . . . Where are they located? . . . Are they pictures or words? . . . Moving, or still?

As you notice your thoughts, notice yourself noticing them. Be aware that you are Observing Yourself. There are your thoughts . . . and there you are, noticing them.

If you can observe your thoughts, then you cannot be your thoughts. You are not your thoughts.

Notice how your thoughts change. They are always changing. Sometimes they are happy, sometimes sad . . . sometimes positive, sometimes not . . . sometimes they are about the past, sometimes about the future. Your thoughts are transient, moving through your mind like a gentle breeze through the trees.

Your thoughts are changing, but the you that notices your thoughts does not change—never changes. As a child, your thoughts were different. But the you who noticed your thoughts as a child is the same you who notices your thoughts today. You are constant.

And if your mind pushes back on this idea . . . allow it to do so. It's just doing its job. See if you can allow those thoughts to come and go, like passing clouds. If your mind tries to pull you away, see if you can return to this exercise. Notice the thoughts, notice your mind distracting you . . . and notice who is noticing.

Now take a moment to notice your body. Notice where your feet make contact with the ground . . . where your legs and back make contact with the chair. And as you observe your body, notice your awareness, that you are the one observing your body.

If you can observe your body, then you cannot be your body. You are not your body.

You have had this body your entire life. Yet over the years, your body has changed. Your cells regenerate so that you are no longer the same physical being as you were when you were born. Your body looks and feels differently than it did as a child. But the you who notices your body is the same. Your awareness never changes. You are constant.

Now bring your awareness to the role you're playing right now. In this moment, perhaps you identify as a business owner. At other times, perhaps you've identified yourself as a client. You may also have identified yourself as a parent, a child, or a partner. A neighbor, a student, or a teacher. A friend, an employer, or an employee.

As you notice the role you are in, notice the Observer Self, the you who is doing the noticing.

If you can observe this role, then you cannot be this role. You are not the role you play.

Each of these is a role you've assumed, and these roles change constantly. And there are some roles you will never be again. You will never be a young child again. But the Observer Self, the you who observes, never changes. You are constant.

You are constant, like the sky. Your thoughts, your emotions, your body, your roles . . . these are the weather. The weather may bring clouds and storms that obstruct the sky, but the sky doesn't change or leave. The sky is always there. You are always there. You are constant.

Your Personal Theater

The following exercise is my own creation, and influenced by guided meditations I've heard and experienced in the past.

To begin, take a comfortable seated position and, when you're ready, close your eyes or lower your gaze.

Start by taking a slow deep breath, inhaling fully, and exhaling fully. Take three deep breaths, and center your attention on your body. Notice how it feels as you breathe in and breathe out. Feel the air as it enters your body through your nostrils, and how it's drawn down into your lungs. Notice your abdomen expanding with the in-breath, and how it gently falls with the out-breath. Become aware of the breath as it leaves your body, and how the air is warmer as it exits.

Now, allow your breath to return to its normal rhythm. Imagine that you are sitting in a darkened movie theater. You are alone in the theater as the film begins to play. You realize that this is no ordinary movie, but instead it is a film of your life. You are watching yourself on screen, going through your life.

On your seat is a remote control. You are able to rewind and fast-forward the film, so that you can watch the moments of your life up until this very moment. You rewind the film and go back to your first day of school. You watch yourself getting ready for the first day of class. Notice what you're doing. Perhaps you're wearing a new outfit, or packing up the backpack you picked out especially for your first day of school.

You're also noticing how you feel. Maybe you're excited, or nervous, or confused as you get ready for school. You're wondering what it will be like to go to school, and what it will be like to have a teacher and friends at school. What will it be like to leave your home and the people who care for you, and spend all day away from them? You spend a few minutes here, watching your younger self get ready and go to your first day of school.

You fast-forward the film until you arrive at your teenage years. You notice everything about yourself as a teenager. You see your friends and family through your teenage eyes. You remember the music you loved, and the relationships that brought you pain. You remember feeling stressed about school or a job. You remember how intense every emotion felt. You spend a few minutes watching your teenage self on the screen.

Then you fast-forward to your early adult years and watch yourself on the screen. What role are you playing here? Notice the people in your life and how you relate to them. Notice the thoughts and feelings that arise as you step back into your early adult years. Spend a few minutes here with your young adult self.

Now, fast-forward the movie so that you're close to present day. Perhaps you're watching yourself from last month, or last week, or maybe even yesterday. Notice everything that's going on in your world. Who are the main characters in your life today? How are you spending your time? What role are you playing in this film today?

Notice that in the film of your life, every scene is connected. From your earliest childhood years, into your adolescence, into your emerging adulthood, and into today. Everything is seamlessly connected to tell the story of your life, and you are watching it unfold before you. You are the Observer, and you have always been the Observer.

In the film of your life, you experience many changes. Your appearance changes as you grow from childhood into adulthood. Your tastes in music, food, and people change. Your best friends in school may no longer be your best adult friends, and your relationships may have changed as well. These changes are a normal part of your life.

Yet through the film, there's one thing that hasn't changed, and that is you. You, the Observer, remain constant. The you who watches the film, who observes your life, remains the same. You've always been here, watching the film of your life, from your earliest memories until today. This you—the Observer Self—will never change.

From this perspective, you realize that in the film of your life, you are the audience, and the actor, and the director, and the producer. You have the power to create your film's narrative and bring it to life. And as you do, you will be watching the story unfold.

You fast-forward the film to the present moment, where you see yourself in the theater, watching the movie of your life. As you rise to leave the theater, you know that the next action you take is up to you and that you are directing the next scene in your film. And you also know that your Observer Self remains in the theater, watching the film you are creating.

CONCLUSION

Here you are, at the end of the book. And while you're still the same you that you've always been, you end this book with a deeper understanding of who you are and how you interact with the world. You're able to view yourself through the lens of entrepreneurial flexibility, and if you've been applying the techniques in Section Two, your business (and your life!) looks and feels extraordinarily different than it did before you read this book.

You are now, and always will be, at a state of choice. You have the knowledge, the talent, and the tools to go out and create whatever you want for your business, your relationships, and your life. You know what's most important to you, and you know how to create and implement a plan to bring your vision to life. You know what to do when your thoughts and emotions threaten to derail you, and you know how to bring yourself back to the present moment, fully aware and connected. Because in the end, the present moment is all we have and everything we have.

Steven Hayes, one of the founders of ACT, developed a metaphor called Passengers on the Bus, and I want to close this book by sharing my version of it with you. You can find a recorded version of this at https://www.actonyourbusiness.com, or may choose to read it to yourself, silently or out loud. It is a lovely example of how the six core processes work together to help us live our lives with intention, purpose, and value. It also illustrates how challenging it can be to put these processes into practice, and tap into the deep pain associated with playing small and allowing our inner trolls to run the show. Different ACT practitioners have adapted this metaphor (for example, Russ Harris refers to his version as Demons on the Boat), but the underlying message is the same: We all have our own private battles, but there is always a way forward.

PASSENGERS ON THE BUS

Each one of us is gifted with our very own bus. I have one, you have one, your terrible ex has one—everyone has a bus. In your bus, you are the driver. You decide where you're going and how you're getting there. Outside the bus is the external world. The people in our lives are out there, each driving their own bus, and the road represents the path we're choosing to take in our lives.

As you drive the bus, your job is to pick up passengers. In this bus, your passengers are not people; after all, every person is already driving their own bus. In this bus, your passengers are everything that goes on in your inner world: the thoughts, feelings, memories, impulses, urges, desires, and sensations you experience. So if you have a memory about your first love, the person you loved is not your passenger. Rather, the memory and feelings evoked by that experience are.

Some of the passengers on your bus are kind, or quiet, or reading a book and minding their own business. But other passengers are loud, intrusive, obnoxious, or downright scary. They scream and throw things, they threaten to hurt you if you don't take them where they want to go, and they make life inside the bus really unpleasant. So you've made a deal with them: You'll go where they want, and they'll quiet down.

You've spent much of your time driving the passengers where they tell you to, and some of these destinations are not ones you would have chosen. Looking out the windshield, you see all sorts of places you'd rather go, and you decide you don't want to chauffeur your passengers anymore. You want to drive your own route.

In a moment of courage, you change course and start toward the destination of your choice. When you do, those nasty passengers get loud and start yelling at you, threatening to tear you apart and destroy you. It gets terrible pretty quickly, so you turn the bus around and return to taking your passengers where they want to go.

And yet, you still see all of these great options in front of you. You could go to the beach, or the mountains, or the lake, or the city. But you're not going there because the passengers have bullied you into going where they want to go, and you feel terrible about it—until you remember the white line.

Every bus has a white line separating the driver from the passengers, and the sign clearly states: "Passengers may not cross the white line while the bus is in motion." So no matter how loud the passengers get, or how much they threaten to hurt you, they can't touch you. They can't harm you. They cannot cross the white line. So you grip the wheel and start driving in the direction of your dreams.

And those passengers rage against you. They create a circle behind your seat and say all sorts of terrible things to you. As you continue to drive toward your destination, you realize that it's all words, and you still have control of the bus. The passengers continue to try to intimidate you, and you keep driving your route. As you do, you realize the passengers are not nearly as big and scary as you thought they were. It's almost as if they were using special effects to make themselves seem bigger and scarier than they actually are.

While you continue driving, you see the landscape stretch out in front of you. There's the sky, and the mountains, and the ocean, and the sun. There are other people driving their buses, and an entire world outside your bus to explore. And you can go anywhere you want—because you're driving the bus.

To Create Space from the passengers, you can name each passenger as they come up. Maybe there's an "I'm not talented enough" passenger, or a passenger that looks like your fourth-grade teacher who tells you that you'll never amount to anything. And as you name them, they step into the sunlight and maybe you see they aren't as big as you thought. Or maybe they now sound like they've sucked helium, which isn't nearly as scary.

Even still, there may be some passengers who continue to scare you. That's okay. You are choosing to Let it Be as you continue toward your destination, even with those uncomfortable feelings.

As you drive, you are aware of the sun streaming through the windshield. You see the road stretch out in front of you and notice the horizon line where the land meets the sky. Everything outside the bus is real and vibrant, and you Anchor Yourself in the moment.

You see all of the other buses out there—all the other drivers driving their routes—and recognize that each bus is filled with that driver's passengers. You sense that every driver has their own struggle, and while some are still choosing to drive their passengers' routes, some have chosen their own course. You feel connected to all of the drivers as you Observe Yourself, realizing that you are creating your route, you are driving your route, and you are fully aware that you are driving.

As you drive, you Determine What Matters by keeping your eyes on the road ahead, focusing your attention on the real world around you and deciding where you want to go. You Make it So by keeping your hands on the wheel and your foot on the gas, moving forward. You are in complete control of where you want to go. And you are excited for the journey.

NEXT STEPS

You have everything you need to create the business and life you want. You've always had it within you, and now with the six core processes of entrepreneurial flexibility in your toolkit, you know exactly what to do to bring your vision to life.

Even though we're at the end of the book, the journey doesn't end here. I've created plenty of additional resources, PDFs, audio guides, and more over at the ACT on Your Business website, which you can access at https://www.actonyourbusiness.com. You can also follow me on Facebook or Instagram at @caravelcoaching to learn more about working with me. Or send me an email at lee@caravel-coaching.com and let me know how the core processes are working for you. I would love to hear from you!

Now get out there and ACT on Your Business. I can't wait to see what you create.

ENDNOTES

1. "Jon Kabat-Zinn: Defining Mindfulness," https://www.mindful.org/jon-kabat-zinn-defining-mindfulness/.

2. Russ Harris, *Act Made Simple: An Easy-to-Read Primer on Acceptance and Commitment Therapy* (New Harbinger Publications), p. 12.

3. You can watch it at https://www.ted.com/talks/simon_sinek_how_great_leaders_inspire_action.

4. Facebook's Investor Relations website, https://investor.fb.com/resources/default.aspx.

5. *Teen Titans Go!*, Season 2, Episode 10, "Slumber Party." Written by Ben Joseph.

6. Brené Brown, Listening to Shame, TED Talk: https://www.ted.com/talks/brene_brown_listening_to_shame.

7. In the Appendix, I've included a version of the Wheel of Life from the Institute of Professional Excellence in Coaching (iPEC).

8. Robert Nozick, *Anarchy, State, and Utopia* (Basic Books).

9. If you don't have a therapist but want to find one, I highly recommend the "Find a Therapist" tool on the *Psychology Today* website (www.psychologytoday.com).

10. Harris, *Act Made Simple*, p. 157.

11. Ibid., p. 177.

Wheel of Life

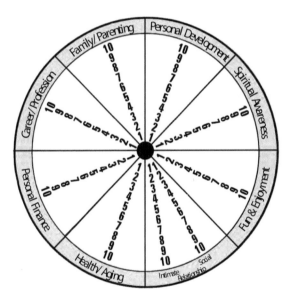

Directions: For each section of the wheel, circle the number that represents your current level of satisfaction. The higher the number, the more satisfied you are in that area.

ACKNOWLEDGMENTS

I wrote this book as a love letter to entrepreneurs and small business owners, and it is only because I have been loved and supported by so many that it exists.

I am immensely grateful to my editor, Jodi Brandon of Jodi Brandon Editorial. Without your wisdom, patience, and encouragement, this concept never would have blossomed from a seed of an idea to a fully blossomed book. I could not have done this without you. Should we do it again?!?

To my coach, Carrie Doubts of Life's Next Chapter Coaching. Great coaches have great coaches, and I have one of the best. Thank you for shepherding me through an extraordinary transformation and helping me achieve my dream.

To Lisa Von De Linde, of LisaVdesigns. You not only created a stunning cover, but you brought such thoughtful beauty to my text. Thank you!

Balša Delibašić, thank you for your care and expertise in indexing, and for helping my readers find exactly what they need at the turn of a page.

I am forever indebted to my team of beta readers: Rachel Allen, Amy James, Reina Pomeroy, Becca Stewart, and Emily Walker. Your energy, insight, and careful attention helped take this book from good to great. I'm so grateful you're a part of my krewe.

Additional thanks to Reina Pomeroy for her skillful coaching and support. This book will help so many more entrepreneurs because of your guidance.

Thank you to the Fueled with Heart community (particularly my fellow Social Glueys!), led by Reina Pomeroy, to the Courage and Clarity Community (particularly my fellow Crickets!), led by Steph Crowder, and to the women of the Spangdahlem OCSC.

To the women of Coastal Women's Forum, I am so grateful to you for being my accountability partners! Special thanks to Sandy Eichelberger, Jane Maulucci, Becca Moorer, and Eileen Nonemaker.

This book never would have existed were it not for my experience as a psychotherapist trained in Acceptance and Commitment Therapy. Thank you to Robyn Walser, who conducted my training almost 10 years ago, and to James Gillies, who served as my traineeship mentor. My life has been forever changed because of both of you.

Thank you to the Institute of Professional Excellence in Coaching (iPEC), particularly Bruce D Schneider, Luke Iorio, Cindy Gardner, Stacy Hartmann, Nina Cashman, Kyle Pertuis, Sherri Gerek, John Bond, and Susan King. Special thanks to my cohort of coaches, particularly Pam Burgess, Kavita Gupta, Alice Schoonbroodt, and Tammy Johnston. You all have changed my life.

Thank you to all of my clients and colleagues. Each of you helped make me a better therapist and stronger coach.

I get by with a little help from my friends, including Nicole Ballinger, Donna Burrowes, Jen Cherry, Jenny Nicholson Cude, Mia Geisinger, Emily & Mike Genest, Sindee Gozansky, Maggie Andrews Miller, Parveen Shamsi Murray, Shana Oakes, Cecilia Ragland Perry, Heather Powell, Dax & Melanie Presuto, Dana Tate Repak, Michelle Ries & Matthew Kinney, Tia Scott & Brandon Shaver, Erin Smith, Beth Troutman Whaley, and Melody Wilding.

Susan Williams, you have been there through every moment of this book's life. I am so grateful for your support, love, and faith in me. Thank you.

Gene & Helen Katz, Rob & Emily Katz, Jay & Cindi Katz, Erin & Josh Howard, and everyone in the Katz and Bleakley clans – I love you all so much. Thank you for being my home base.

To my children, Jack and Ben. Being your mom is the best job in the world. Thank you for bringing joy into my life.

And finally, to my heart, Patrick. None of this would be possible without you. I love you so much.

INDEX

ABOUT THE AUTHOR

Lee Chaix McDonough, LCSW, MSPH, ACC, is a business coach, licensed clinical social worker, and founder of Caravel Coaching. She is a proud alumna of the University of North Carolina at Chapel Hill, where she received her bachelor degrees in Psychology and Dramatic Art, and her Master of Social Work and Master of Science in Public Health degrees. For over a decade, Lee provided therapy and social work services in a variety of settings, including hospitals, local government, non-profit, the Department of Veterans Affairs, and as a civilian for the United States Air Force. She transitioned into business coaching, and now works with helpers, healers, and creative entrepreneurs as they create, grow, and scale successful business while remaining true to their vision and values.

Lee lives in New Bern, North Carolina with her husband, Patrick, and their children, Jack and Ben. Learn more about her at caravelcoaching.com or actonyourbusiness.com, or connect with her on Instagram at @caravelcoaching.

Made in the USA
Thornton, CO
12/05/22 15:15:19